MORE PR.
ALTA FAY'S ALLEGIANCE

"This is the beautiful and eloquent story of two small-town girls who faced everything that life threw at them-and thrived. It is the story of a country on the verge of losing itself, only to rediscover its own values–just as the Blanchard sisters discover the meaning of life during the worst, and best, of American times."

—**Wilma Askinas**, author of *A Splice of Life*

"Deftly weaves fiction with facts: mentioning President Hoover, Franklin D. Roosevelt, the WPA, Prohibition, and songs from the Great Depression. Graceful, evocative, a masterpiece!"

—**Pat Moffett**, author of *Fortunate Soldier*

"A stunning debut novel that will instantly transport you back in time. This fabulous author has written an achingly-beautiful first novel. It has been years since I read a book that moved me the way Alta Fay's Allegiance did."

—**Eldon Thomas**, author of *Table for Three*

ALTA FAY'S ALLEGIANCE

Amber Ellis

Most of the names and places in this story have been changed. Alta Fay's Allegiance is loosely based on a true story.

HARDSCRABBLE
PUBLISHING

Alta Fay's Allegiance
by Amber Ellis

Copyright © 2005 by Amber Ellis
Hardscrabble Publishing

All rights reserved. No part of this book may be reproduced (except for inclusion in reviews), disseminated or utilized in any form or by any means, electronic or mechanical, including photocopying, recording, or in any information storage and retrieval system, or the Internet/World Wide Web without written permission from the author or publisher.

For further information, contact the author at:
Hardscrabble Publishing
P.O. Box 973
Lewiston, MI 49756

Book Design by:
The Floating Gallery
244 Madison Avenue, #254
New York, NY 10016
www.thefloatinggallery.com

Alta Fay's Allegiance
Amber Ellis

1. Author 2. Title 3. Memoir

Library of Congress Control Number 2005926285
ISBN 0-9768591-0-6 (paperback)

Back Cover Photo by Studio 131, Inc.

Photographs and artwork by Amber Ellis

This book is dedicated to:
JC MYLAS

*The many men and women who
discussed their Depression experiences with me.*

*My family
Grandma Miss Mouse (Phyllis)
Archie B. Wicks (Phyllis's husband of 51 years)
Jim Miesen, and Diane Marlatt.*

*God Bless All of You!
Thank you*

CONTENTS

Foreward vii
Chapter 1–Troubled Times 1
Chapter 2–Black and White, Shades of Gray 12
Chapter 3–Getting Along 19
Chapter 4–The Good, the Bad,
 and the Chance to Succeed 26
Chapter 5–Early Summer 29
Chapter 6–Judy 38
Chapter 7–Grandpa's Surprise 45
Chapter 8–Old Mattie Squires 50
Chapter 9–Dottie 58
Chapter 10–Narrow Escape 61
Chapter 11–Death 65
Chapter 12–Grandpa and the Farmers' Almanac 69
Chapter 13–The Pocketknife 75
Chapter 14–The Cold Winter 79
Chapter 15–Snow Days 84
Chapter 16–The Storm 87
Chapter 17–A Sorrowful Journey Home 94

Chapter 18–Memories of Days Gone By 102
Chapter 19–Grief 110
Afterwards 123
Epilogue 126
Author's Note 131

FOREWARD

When I interviewed individuals about their personal recollections of the Great Depression, the first thing many would say was, "Oh, you should have spoken with Eunice or Grandma or the Beverly sisters. They could really have given you some interesting information about that time."

Unfortunately, these witnesses are often deceased. Indeed, with each passing year we are left with fewer first-hand, adult experiences of that generation. It is my belief, however, that those who were children during this period do not give themselves enough credit. While it is true that their parents sheltered them from the day-to-day adult responsibilities, these children often helped their families with crucial necessities. A child's point of view may be colored by innocence, but Depression-era children provide a unique and invaluable perspective.

The one statement consistent to the children or young adults of the Great Depression era is this: "We were poor but didn't know it." It was repeated verbatim throughout the many interviews I conducted, and I attribute the sentiment to the solid, loving parents, grandparents, and good neighbors of these Depression-era children.

Once again, the faith, perseverance, hard work, and determination of these families demonstrate why America is still considered the greatest nation on Earth.

I am thankful for their efforts and willingness to share their memories with me. Their personal memories and experiences are incapable of being reproduced exactly as they happened, but through their aged and tired eyes, I hope to have captured enough feeling and vision to recreate a story that represents the lives of one poor family during this trying time.

Do not forget or neglect the older generation. These people have lived through several devastating wars, the Great Depression, and lightning speed technological advances. They have experienced riding in a horse and buggy, and traveling by train, automobile, and jet. They have used the telegraph, switchboard, radio, television, computer, and cell phone. They've lit their way with kerosene lanterns, batteries, and electric lights. They ran outside into the cold winter night to use the outhouse. They drew water from open wells and flowing springs. They went from having to wear handmade, printed grain-sack dresses and bloomers to shopping on-line. Their knowledge, wisdom, and experiences are more precious than gold. Listen to their stories. They have wonderful and interesting stories to share. Let them know that they are loved, appreciated, respected, and irreplaceable. Enjoy their company while you can. Our lives are like drops of water in the ocean of Forever. We must make them meaningful.

Amber Ellis

Pencil Drawing by Amber Ellis

Chapter 1

Troubled Times

AN ARTIST'S PALETTE OF BRILLIANT colors vainly chased the setting sun as dusk overtook the sky. The late spring evening became chilly as the sky grew to a pale gray. Down the lane, at a distant farm, a lone dog barked. Nearby, sitting on the edge of an old dirt road, a whippoorwill trilled its distinct song. The countryside was preparing for a much needed rest after a warm, busy day of renewal.

George sat on the worn-out front porch steps of his shabby, whitewashed home, resting quietly. His elbows poked into his knees. His palms cradled his chin, and stubby, calloused fingers warmed his cheeks. A tremendous weight, with the smothering heaviness of a pitch-black night, pressed mercilessly down on George's broad shoulders. He gazed at, but could not see, nature's masterpiece as evening melted into night. His troubled mind was miles away, briefly escaping into the past, where a better place and happier times abounded. He often tried to remain in this place as long as possible, canceling out the present reality. Unfortunately, the dream always ended abruptly with the screech of a child, the thunderous boom of his wife's tired, angry voice, or the sudden heart-stopping slam of the front porch door. If only he could sleep and dream forever, but they wouldn't let him. Often, he would press his hands tightly to his ears to try and keep the noise out. *Leave me alone!* George's mind screamed. But they wouldn't. They couldn't. It was family life, his family, his responsibility, his everything. Life was battering him from every direction, and George often lashed back in anger. Alcohol would temporarily help, but with Prohibition in full force, his drug of choice was scarce. Cigarettes would have to suffice in taking the edge off. But they cost money; numbing his senses with dreaming cost nothing, if only he would be left alone.

There was little work to be found in the few years following the Stock Market Crash of '29. Some men he knew had deserted their families for a time. They left them with the hope that the apparent abandonment would bring relief aid to their rescue. These men lived as grungy hobos on smelly, insect- and-rodent-infested boxcars. They traveled from one destitute place to another. As awful as the hobo life was, a knot of guilt twisted inside George for envying these men's lives. George had tasted war. Rough living conditions were not new to him. Filth did not frighten him, because it was only himself he needed to look after. He set his own pace and did as he pleased.

He knew it was selfish of him to think this way. He should appreciate all he had been given. But he couldn't. Having a family was a much different assignment indeed. Keeping it together was more difficult than being a combat soldier. *Am I strong enough for this life-long tour of duty?* George often wondered.

George reasoned that he would be a decent man who, once he found a job, would send for his family. Many men had shared George's gallant attitude. But given the chance at the single life again with very little responsibility, these once gallant-minded men never came back home. As burdened as he was, George still loved his family, though outwardly it was not consistently evident. Thus, he did not leave his family for fear of what he may do once set free from his present obligations. He did not trust himself. He expected he would act as a man of integrity and send for his family, but he wasn't completely convinced. His family had raised him to accept responsibility; he would not have it be said one day that he chose the cowardly way out. So George remained home. Like it or not, it was all he knew. He was not a man of chance. He would not step out of his comfort zone, for fear of discovering the man he might truly be. Life had left him scared, hurt, and angry. In so many ways he had become a bitter man. Yet it hadn't always been that way. And those dreams of better days became his numbing consolation.

A steady income during these tumultuous times was rare. The odd jobs and small amount of trapping George did brought in little money for his growing family. He was a simple man with a seventh-grade education who had honorably fought in World War I. He returned home, physically and mentally exhausted from witnessing the atrocities of war, to marry his childhood sweetheart, Mary Blanchard. By 1931 they had been blessed with seven healthy children: Barbara, Clare, Phyllis, Alta Fay, Jonathon, Matthew, and baby Michael.

Phyllis and Alta Fay were close in age, and one was seldom found without the other by her side. Phyllis was strong, both physically and mentally. Her golden brown hair framed her soft, round, lady-like face. She had an angelic aura about her that no one could explain. Both adults and children alike were inevitably drawn to her warm, comforting personality. Mary, the girls' mother, relied heavily on Phyllis to help care for the younger siblings. She was a dependable, loving caregiver and a hard worker.

Alta Fay, one year younger than Phyllis, was thin, gangly, and athletic. Her features were sharper than those of Phyllis, and she was more outspoken and carefree. She was the daredevil of the Clayton children. Alta Fay could run like the wind and was always the first chosen when teams were drawn up for baseball in the schoolhouse yard. Everyone enjoyed Alta Fay's friendly, jovial personality. George, like those who knew her, laughed at Alta Fay's silliness. Her natural sense of humor broke up the monotony of the troubled times. It seemed that Alta Fay was the one person who could bring George out of his depressed moods. Like a lifeline, her humor pulled her daddy up and out of the darkness and back into their lives.

On occasion George, Phyllis, and Alta Fay would pile into George's old, beat-up truck and travel across the state line into Ohio. Here they would pick up a variety of dirt-cheap, second-hand items and haul these treasures back to Michigan, where he could peddle them and turn a small profit. These items were available because desperate, poverty-stricken people were forced to sell family heirlooms and other precious items in order to put food on their tables. George detested this business, and he warned his girls never to look back once the items were loaded and they were on their way home. He knew the anguish his dealings caused the families. He could not bear to see their tears. It only added more heavy links to his mile-long chain of guilt. However, he set his jaw firmly and drove on, knowing that he, too, was a desperate man that had an obligation to his own family. He temporarily set his mind at ease, convincing himself, once again, that the end justified the means.

In many ways these were stagnant times. Like a smoldering summer heat wave that made it difficult to breathe, there was a sluggish placidness hanging over the entire country. The economy was muddled, and there seemed to be no light at the end of the tunnel. Fortunately, George Clayton was confident that these hard times would soon end with the presidential election of 1932. However, the election was a year away.

Most folks who were asked adamantly vocalized their unhappiness with the Republican Party and President Herbert Hoover's leadership as president. Hoover's chances of re-election in 1932 were slim to none; he had served a mere eight months in office when the October '29 Crash occurred. "Sure didn't take him long to mess up the county, aye," thought George ignorantly. Like so many of these people, George was hoping that next November's election would go as planned, and that the popular New York Governor, Franklin D. Roosevelt, would be the newly elected President of the United States of America.

With boisterous confidence George bragged out loud to an invisible audience in his front yard: "President-elect Roosevelt will restore prosperity to this tuckered out land. If all that boastin' wasn't just hogwash campaignin' rabble by the Democratic Party, the troubles and sorrows of God's great country will soon be just a bad memory." He grinned sardonically to himself at his own feeble prophecy. How was he to know what would happen in the next few months or even years for that matter? How was anyone to know? *Only the Lord knows and He ain't been sharin' his secrets with me*, thought George, glaring skyward, an unrepentant smirk playing across his weathered face.

As the night patiently listened, George continued to ponder the issues of the day. Mary leaned against the doorframe for a moment, observing her husband from behind the screen door. He looked small and worn out sitting there alone. The Great Depression seemed to age people ten-fold in a short period of time. It broke Mary's heart to see her once strong husband crumbling away. Yet, it made her all the more determined to remain steady and strong. She must trudge through the Depression's muck and come out the other side with her family still intact.

So, like a swimmer, Mary sucked in a deep breath of air and slowly, without a noise, walked out of the warm house into the cold night air. George turned and briefly greeted her with a blank stare. Then, without saying a word, he gave his attention back to the night. Ignoring his indifference, Mary eased herself onto the porch. She carefully handed George a steaming cup of black coffee. It wasn't the store bought type; rather it was dried field corn that had been parched in the oven until it was brown. Mary's mother had taught her to crack it with a hammer, making it as little and as fine as possible, and add it to boiling hot water. Neither George nor Mary particularly cared for this sorry coffee substitute, but they drank it without complaint.

Wrapping her hands tightly around the warm mug, Mary asked, "What you thinkin' on George?"

"Nothing. Nothing you need mind yourself about," George answered coldly. Quickly changing the subject, he commented, "Sure would be nice to have some decent coffee again."

"Sure would be nice havin' a lot of things, George, but we just don't. We'll be all right. Things will get better; you'll see; you just gotta trust the Lord."

George began laughing. "Yeah, he'll provide all right! Ha!"

Mary refused to become angered, although his blasphemy struck her like a punch in the stomach. She silently asked God to forgive her husband; he was tired and didn't really mean what he had said. The worn-out, discouraged couple continued to sit on the porch together. Mary laid her head on George's warm shoulder. He did not object; however, neither did he acknowledge her need for closeness. He was numb inside. He tried to fight it, but lately he was losing the battle. His insides ached. Every part of him was crying, except no tears would come to his eyes. George wished his wife could see how badly he was hurting, but she couldn't seem to understand or know what to do. Night sounds filled the air, but between this couple, on this night, nothing more was said.

Phyllis and Alta Fay found their parents out on the porch and scrambled through the doorway at top speed. Showing off, the girls jumped off the steps from the very top and rolled out into the yard. Their siblings stayed inside where it was warm. The youngest children had already been put to bed. Now, Phyllis and Alta Fay frisked about their scraggly, weed infested lawn, chasing each other like a cat and mouse. Mostly they were showing off for their father, hoping to capture his attention, but he didn't pay them much mind. He continued his attempt at figuring things out in his head and had, once again, withdrawn from the world around him. Phyllis and Alta Fay, tired and aware that their efforts at attracting attention were fruitless, ended their chase and noisily flopped down onto the steps beneath their parents. Using her fingertips, Phyllis quietly brushed a small pile of sand from the step. All the while she wondered when her "old" daddy would come back and set things straight again in their lives.

As if George could read Phyllis's thoughts, he also wondered if it was possible that the turmoil would ever end. Like many fathers, George wanted to be a hero in his children's eyes and a rock solid companion for his wife. However, George felt as if he was failing his entire family. His once broad shoulders were slumped, and his face was dark and expressionless. Phyllis wondered, at times, if her father even liked himself. So much of the time he acted angry toward everyone around him. It had become more difficult to read his ever-changing moods, and he often distanced himself from Mary and the children.

George, stone-faced and staring into the night, instinctively reached into his worn-out shirt pocket and pulled out a pouch of tobacco and a single cigarette paper. In a flash, Phyllis and

Alta Fay both jumped up from their positions on the step and offered, "I'll do that for you Daddy." Their small hands reached out, each one hoping that they would be the lucky winner in retrieving the items.

Instead, George brushed the back of his hairy hand at them. "Go play. Girls shouldn't be rollin' cigarettes for their old man."

The girls had asked because it presented an opportunity to be near their daddy and do something for him. Though it was a trivial task and it assisted in the promotion of a nasty habit, Phyllis and Alta Fay needed some closeness and approval from him, but he continued to push them away. Their well-intended efforts floundered, and they resolved to leave the porch and resume their game of tag.

Back on the porch steps, George meticulously laid the creased wrapper on the porch, centered the tobacco on it in a neat line, rolled it carefully, and licked the paper's edge to seal it. After placing the twisted edge between his lips, he cupped his hand over the end of his cigarette and lit a match. Touching it to the far end for a split second, the end began to glow bright orange. He shook the match until the flame died and tossed the remains into the dirt.

Slowly and smoothly he took a long drag on his cigarette. Then he blew a steady stream of smoke out of his nose and mouth as he gazed up into the darkened sky. It was as if he was blowing his troubles into the night, never to see them again. He wished it were that simple.

Deep inside, Mary was occasionally bitter toward George for spending money on extravagances like cigarettes. But most of the time she was riddled with guilt because her tired husband was providing the best he could for their family, and he deserved at least this luxury. On the other hand, Mary felt that her contributions to their family often went unnoticed. George did not help in this respect. He made sure his wife understood her role as that of the less important person in their marriage. He would often burst out angrily at her. "You have no idea what it's like tryin' to provide for you all." Mary accepted this verbal abuse with humility.

"Sittin' around here with these kids and waitin' for *my* money to be handed over to you," he would say. "Lucky for you if I don't up and leave the whole lot of you." In Mary's mind, it was true. She wasn't the breadwinner and didn't deserve the luxuries like those afforded to George. She could and would do without. Mary was accustomed to the situation but was never truly content with the blatant inequality. In the end, though, she always held her tongue; in order to keep peace in their home, she did not badger him about luxuries and the like.

George finished his cigarette, dropped it onto the porch step, and snuffed it out with the toe of his worn out boot. In silence, he stood up, walked back into the house, washed up, and went to bed without saying good night to any of them. The rest of the family quietly followed.

Late that night the house grew so cold that the girls could see their breath. It was a last ditch effort on the part of Old Man Winter to maintain control of nature. Yet spring would ultimately win the fight. Everyone and everything knew this for a fact. Spring was becoming steadily stronger each day and night. Meanwhile, though, Phyllis and Alta Fay were grateful that their mother had built a fire. They each heated a brick, wrapped it in a towel, and placed them under the covers, down near their feet. Finally, the girls crawled into bed.

"Look, I'm smoking," teased Alta Fay as she pretended to be holding a cigarette. She batted her eyelashes to appear sophisticated then blew a steady imaginary stream of smoke at Phyllis.

"Stop messin' around, Alta," ordered Phyllis. A quiet giggle following. "I'm cold and want to get to sleep."

Alta did as she was told and snuggled with Phyllis beneath their heavy homemade quilt to keep warm. The two said nothing for a long time. The room was pitch black, and the only sound to be heard in this very still night was the tick, tock, tick, tock of the family's grandfather clock, which rested proudly against the wall in the living room.

Without warning, it struck promptly on the half-hour, breaking the silence. Neither of the girls had fallen asleep. There were aspects of this terrible time that affected even the youngest of children.

"Does Daddy not like us anymore, Phil?" Alta Fay's voice was quivering as she spoke softly to her sister. Phyllis did not know what to say. It had startled her when Alta spoke because she was sure Alta was already asleep. Phyllis yawned loudly and rolled over to face her wide-eyed sister. She was not sure why her Daddy had become so disinterested in the family. But Alta's big, blue eyes demanded to know. Phyllis knew she had to come up with an answer, and only an honest answer would satisfy Alta Fay.

Phyllis gently touched Alta Fay's head and caressed her fine hair. "Daddy is trying to find steady work, Alta, and there just doesn't seem to be any. I guess that's why he acts so mad sometimes. He's not mad at us, Alta Fay. He's mad at someone else."

"If I could get a job, I would," said Alta Fay. "I just want him to be happy again."

Phyllis said nothing, but continued to listen to her sister's concerns, though her own eyelids began to droop. She had to blink frequently to stay awake. Just as Phyllis's eyes closed for the night, Alta Fay added forlornly, "Mamma cries a lot, Phil."

Jerking herself out of a dead sleep, Phyllis flatly stated, "I know. These are sad times for her. Daddy isn't very nice to her, and she has all of us kids to take care of." Phyllis's response was both quick and well beyond her years. With more confidence and wakefulness, Phyllis added, "I think we need to help Mamma out as best we can. That would make her *and* Daddy happier, I'll bet."

Alta Fay sighed with satisfaction to Phyllis's comments and suggestions. Suddenly, the long day and chilly night overcame her; she contentedly touched Phyllis's cheek with her soft, tiny fingertips, rolled over and drifted into a dreamless sleep.

Phyllis smiled to herself, draped her arm over Alta Fay and closed her eyes. Sleep came quickly and peacefully.

Time marched slowly on. Late spring became summer and summer turned to fall. Still, times were hard and many continued to suffer.

They used to tell me I was building a dream, and so I followed the mob,
When there was earth to plow, or guns to bear, I was always there right on the job.
They used to tell me I was building a dream, with peace and glory ahead,
Why should I be standing in line, just waiting for bread?

Once I built a railroad, I made it run, made it race against time.
Once I built a railroad; now it's done. Brother, can you spare a dime?

Excerpt from, "Brother, Can You Spare a Dime," lyrics by Yip Harburg, music by Gorney Harburg (1931).

Chapter 2

Late 1931
Black and White, Shades of Gray

UNLIKE THE CLAYTON FAMILY, THE country's Great Depression did not monetarily affect some families. Many self-sufficient farmers seemed to scarcely notice the upheaval of the American society. George was envious of those people, and he found an excuse for feeling sorry for himself. He adamantly claimed that everyone better off than himself had been dealt life's good hand, and he the bad. This type of thinking allowed him to justify his rustling of a sheep every now and then to feed his family. *Surely society would understand that a man must sometimes resort to drastic measures in order to ensure the survival of his family,* reasoned George, knowing good and well this wasn't true, but doing his best to suppress his guilty feelings. Mary would not approve of this behavior, but, as the old saying goes, nothing steps between a mother bear and her cubs or it is in grave danger. She will go to great lengths to ensure the safety of her offspring. Human mothers are quite similar. If it's hunger that steps between a mother and her children, she will accept a food offering without asking where it came from in order to fill her children's empty bellies. Though times were becoming tougher, Mary kept her children in the cozy house, away from the cold barn and 'shades of gray,' where the men were dressing out the rustled sheep. She strove to walk the narrow road, know black and white, assured of absolutes. Mary desired to lead her children this way as well.

One particularly cold, autumn night, Phyllis and Alta Fay lay nestled beneath their covers, unable to sleep peacefully because their bellies were empty. They did not speak to each other, because hunger often makes one ornery and miserable. These girls were both.

The grandfather clock struck eleven times, but this could barely be heard above the rumblings in their stomachs.

They knew that their father had gone out with some friends and hadn't come in until very late. When Alta Fay finally spoke, she asked, "Where'd you think Daddy went?" Without waiting for an answer, she continued, "He's not leavin' us like he always says, is he?"

"No," replied Phyllis. "He's probably helpin' out Mr. Rush. Ma said he doesn't know much 'bout fixin' a broken down truck, but Daddy does."

Alta Fay meekly smiled. "I think our Daddy knows just about everything."

"Yeah," replied Phyllis, in an unconvinced voice. Alta Fay didn't pick up on the hint of sarcasm, but that was for the best. Alta Fay needed to have a hero, and, in a way, George needed to be a hero. He yearned for a vote of confidence; even coming from a youngster it would mean the world to him.

The clock struck the half-hour. It was 11:30, and sleep had still not come to Phyllis. Alta Fay quietly rested. A few moments later, Phyllis instinctively sat up when she heard the back door open and the low murmur of voices. She could hear her father's boots scraping along the hardwood floor. Though very young Phyllis knew the old house well, and she could picture in her mind, just by sound, the exact location of anyone walking about. She could almost see her father and one of his friends, cold and tired, standing in the doorway to the kitchen. She was startled out of her thoughts, however, when she suddenly heard her mother's voice in the mix. Phyllis was so certain that Mamma had gone to bed several hours before that she became slightly embarrassed. Her usual keen sense had not told her that Mamma was still up and about.

Was something wrong? Phyllis wondered as she gently nudged Alta Fay. Waking from a light sleep, Alta Fay rubbed her eyes and turned to face Phyllis.

"What's wrong?" Alta asked sleepily.

"That's what I'm wondering," replied Phyllis, anxiously. Nightmarish thoughts raced through Phyllis's mind. *Did someone get hurt? Was it Uncle Allen or Uncle Frank? Was it Grandma or Grandpa Blanchard?* The thoughts pounded her head like a fist. Without saying a word, Phyllis pulled Alta Fay out of bed. Looking into her younger sister's face, she pressed her index finger to her lips to create the "keep quiet" gesture, and slipped out from behind the curtain that separated their bedroom from the kitchen. They fitted themselves in easily between the wood box and the wall. It was a great hide-and-seek spot. The children used it often in their play. They just knew that their mother had no idea about this secret hiding place. So it was the most logical vantage point from which to hear what was going on. Phyllis had been taught that it was not polite to be eavesdropping, but she was as curious as Alta Fay was adventurous. If caught, they could always say that they were frightened that something bad had happened to someone they knew. At least it would not be a lie.

"I need a big pan for the meat," George demanded. "It was a big sheep we got tonight, so I gave Elmer the hind quarter for helpin' me out."

Peering over the top of the old wood box, the girls could see their mother frowning. The few wrinkles she had were vivid, showing great worry. "George, you know I don't like this. My family ain't crooks," Mary said proudly.

George looked tired, and the girls could see that he was beginning to get upset. A sarcastic smile stretched across his face as he defensively stated, "Well, well, the Blanchard's are sure saintly aren't they. Well, this heathen Clayton is tryin' to keep his kids fed, and I'll do it any way I know how!" The children were afraid that he might hit their mother with the back of his strong hand. His bellowing, angry voice brought tears to their eyes. However, Mary remained calm, said nothing in reply, and went to where she stored her pots and pans.

As Mary handed him a mammoth sized silver pan, she attempted to explain. "You know what I mean, George. It's stealin' and it's breakin' the Lord's commandment." Her lips tightly pursed, she intentionally smoothed out the front of her apron. Though there was not a wrinkle to be found, this helped to relieve the tension she was feeling. Mary's eyes were glued to his.

Looking down at his boots, George haughtily replied, "Well, you'll just have to ask for some forgiveness for the both of us then, cause I got me a sheep to cut up. If He ain't providin', then I've got to. He can't begrudge a man that."

Mary turned her head away in an attempt to ignore her husband's blasphemous talk. Yet the truth was that their children were hungry. She could not let her pride cause them all pain. Relenting, Mary quietly walked to her sink and began methodically placing her clean, dry dishes into the cupboard.

With the pan tucked under his arm, he hesitated, turned to Mary and reasoned more gently. "The guy has at least a hundred sheep; he ain't gonna miss one." Without another word George again lowered his head and clomped out the back door. It slammed behind him, startling Mary and the stealthy eavesdroppers.

She stood staring at the water-stained ceiling, hugging her stomach. It looked as if she had a terrible stomachache. But it went even deeper than a physical ailment. It went straight to her heart. Those last words from her husband had struck discord in her mind. She was reminded of a Bible story. She felt uneasy, yet could not dispute George's logic.

Does a farmer know if one of his hundred sheep is missing? She knew of one Shepherd that did. The subject was quickly becoming too complex, and Mary was getting tired, eager to get the meat taken care of so she could go to bed. Presently, she thought no more of the matter.

Meanwhile, the young, wide-eyed eavesdroppers continued to follow their mamma's every move. It seemed as if the world was holding its breath. Finally, Mary lowered herself into a chair at the kitchen table. She clasped her callused hands in prayer and rested her forehead on her thumbs. She rested for such a long time that the girls thought their mother had fallen asleep. They remained absolutely silent.

Mary's eyes were not shut due to sleep, but in honest reverence. "Dear Lord, you know how hungry the children are. Please forgive George and me for breaking your commandment," she softly spoke aloud.

After a moment, she looked up. Her eyes were moist with tears as she looked about her lonely kitchen. All at once, Mary's stare fell directly on two sets of innocent, concerned eyes. Mother had honed in on her target as stealthily as a fighter pilot. How she did this would baffle Phyllis until she had children of her own.

Mary casually leaned back in her chair, folded her arms, and said, "You two snoopers get out here right now."

Slowly and clumsily both girls crawled out from their hiding place. They feared that mamma would give them a swat with her wooden spoon. It would have been warranted, Phyllis knew. Once the children were put to bed it was expected that they would remain there without question.

Instead, Mary gestured for the girls to sit with her at the table.

Timidly they obeyed. Pulling out their chairs, the girls never took their sober eyes off of Mamma. Using their hands to find where the seats were, they carefully sat down. Mary knew that the girls were sorry for eavesdropping and was not angry with them. However, when she finally spoke, she had a little fun pretending to be mad.

"How long have you two been spyin' on your daddy and me?" she asked harshly, looking slyly out of the corner of her eyes at her offenders.

Phyllis spoke up first. "We couldn't sleep and then I heard Daddy come in and then I heard you and wondered what you were doing up so late and…" Phyllis stammered, feeling concerned and embarrassed for disobeying her parents.

"Whoa, Phil. Calm down," Mamma tenderly said as she wrapped her hand around Phyllis's arm and gently squeezed. "It's hard to sleep when your belly is rumbling. Your daddy's gotten us some meat." She smiled meekly, not divulging any more information.

If you girls aren't too sleepy yet, maybe you could help me cut it up," mamma suggested.

Eager to be of any help and avoiding punishment, the girls said in unison, "Sure."

After about fifteen minutes, George hauled in the heavy pan of bloody meat. At first, George had eyed his girls with surprise and curiosity, but did not scold them for being up.

Instead, he looked to Mary and said, "There is still about one more pan to be brought in."

Mary went to her cupboard once more and found another pan. She smiled as she handed it to George. Before he walked out the door, he turned to his girls and said, "You're up to help out your ma, not to be messin' around." With a hint of a grin, he left to the barn once more.

It was only a couple of hours before the meat was completely taken care of. Mary fried several pieces for all of them to snack on. The aroma wafting through the kitchen made them all the more hungry. It was difficult to be patient until the meat finished frying. Mamma didn't need to bother waking the other children because they were in the kitchen the moment the lovely scent drifted into their cold rooms. Jonathon and Matthew stood on tiptoe, eagerly wanting whatever smelled so good. The older girls smiled and helped their mother serve some of the meat to the rest of the family. Mary would also make the family a big pan of meat for their breakfast. It would be a wonderful treat to wake up to. With thankful smiles, contented stomachs, and a kiss for both their parents, the midnight scavengers were finally ready for a long, peaceful sleep. Phyllis and Alta Fay had helped out their mother tremendously and allowed her to retire to bed much earlier than expected.

Chapter 3

Getting Along

RUSTLED SHEEP AND OTHER QUESTIONABLE activities provided evidence that right and wrong had become blurry during the depression. It appeared to be most hazy for those families who did not have a solid spiritual foundation. Mary tried to maintain the highest level of virtue that she could, but George was a bit more flexible. This became obvious as the family's troubles continued, and George's frustrations heightened.

The bitterly cold fall of '31 had quickly drained the Clayton's small supply of coal, and George's family was now hungry, cold, and without money. One late evening, George shared his predicament with his wife.

"I've already cut all the dried limbs down, and cut off trees along the road for the fire, but there is no more." Mary was rocking Matthew to sleep. She remained hollow-eyed, not able to offer George any answers. He knew she couldn't help out in this respect. He was just sharing his troubles with her. Why did it seem that when he wanted to talk, Mary didn't; when George didn't feel like talking, Mary did? This partnership was one that George thought he would probably never be able to figure out.

Early the next morning, George swallowed his pride and walked down to the town supervisor's office and asked if some coal could be brought to the house. The man in charge turned George down. He was shocked and angry that they had refused to help him. In a rage he walked back home at a brisk and determined pace. In George's feisty, fighting manner, he told Mary directly that he had decided to cut down the huge elm tree out in the county's right-of-way next to the road. He followed through with his threat.

As soon as word traveled back to the supervisor, a spindly, beady-eyed man wearing round wire-rimmed glasses came to the home and said to George in his most authoritative, but squeaky voice, "You know, you could be arrested for cuttin' that tree down." Pointing his long, bony finger in the direction of the stump, the weasel of a man shifted nervously from one foot to the other, not sure how George would react. Rumor had it that George could get violent when cornered, and this small squeaker wasn't in a hurry to find out if it was true.

George glanced toward the fallen elm then back to the weasel and staunchly replied, "Well, we needed wood. I had to keep the kids, the family, warm. If you want to put me in jail for that then it's all right with me. I'll be havin' my meals and be in a warm jail 'cause I'm gonna keep right on cutting."

With that stated matter-of-factly, George turned back, paying no more attention to the weasel man, and resumed cutting the gigantic elm into firewood.

In a haughty manner, the man straightened to his full height, stuck his nose into the air, and stomped off to his car. Surprisingly, the next day a truck arrived that had a load of coal on it for the Clayton's. It was like a load of diamonds had just been given to them. And though that was the end of this particular incident, it was not the end of the hard times. They were still coming like a runaway locomotive. At a fast and furious pace, they were demolishing anyone or anything in their path.

Late October was cold and dreary. Many days the sky remained a pasty gray. One afternoon, two of Phyllis's bachelor uncles, Allen and Frank, came over while George was away working on a garage in town for a local carpenter. These uncles checked in on their favorite sister quite often because they enjoyed her friendly company and strong coffee. Mary was not the tidiest housekeeper, and her kitchen table was always cluttered with coffee mugs, the salt and pepper shakers, crumbs from the morning's toast, and tidbits of this and that that the children added to it over the course of the day. Yet the cleanest kitchen in the county could not hold a candle to Mary's warm friendly kitchen. Many people, like her own brothers, were drawn to this comfortable, welcoming place.

The sibling trio sat sipping some black coffee and chatting about the town gossip and major events in the country, when Mamma commented, "We haven't had meat in some time. The last of the veal has been gone for some time. I'm not sure when and if things are ever going to get better." She wasn't expecting her brothers to have an answer for her. It was just her way of relieving some pent up concerns.

However, after a few moments of thinking, Allen replied, "We know where a nest of rabbits are living. They're in a culvert down the road a ways." Mary looked wide-eyed from one brother then to the other. This was wonderful news. Though it sounded as if she was asking for a handout, she was glad she had mentioned their predicament. Immediately Allen and Frank grabbed their caps, kissed Mary on the forehead, thanked her for the coffee, and said they would return soon. They took a burlap sack from the shed, jumped into their old truck, and headed off to help out their sister and her kids.

"You don't think George is gonna be mad, do you?" Frank asked his brother.

"I don't care if he is. Those kids are hungry. He'll just have to get over it," replied Allen, without remorse.

In a short while, they pulled the truck into the high brown weeds along the edge of an isolated dirt road. The truck was stopped but a second when Allen dashed out and stationed himself at one end of the culvert with the sack. Quicker than one could say Jack Robinson, Uncle Frank was at the other end with a long stick. Frank poked around in the culvert until the rabbits became frightened and ran into the sack Uncle Allen was holding. Once in the burlap bag, Allen tied it tight and held it up in triumph. "Gottem!" he yelled.

"Good work," said Frank. "Let's get going before someone comes along and catches us!"

They proudly carried three large jackrabbits back to their sister. She was obliged to have them do the dirty work of killing the rabbits, but she would skin and cook them. It was just a short time when the homey kitchen was filled with the aroma of golden brown, crispy fried rabbit meat. The children all smiled and chattered as they devoured the delicious meal. After saving George a plateful of fried rabbit, Mary used the extra meat, adding it to some stock, and slow cooked it for a rabbit stew for tomorrow's meal. Forgetting their manners, they noisily licked their greasy fingers when they had finished.

"Boy, that was awful kind of you guys," thanked Mary, smiling as she cleared the table and began to boil a kettle of water for the girls to do the dishes with.

Allen sipped another cup of Mary's strong black coffee and replied, "Aw, those rug rats need some meat now and again. We're glad to help out."

"It was a fine meal for us as well, sis," Frank laughed and continued, "Yeah, I think we'll go to Ma's tomorrow night for our next dinner! We're on a roll, Allen!" The trio laughed and the kids smiled, not really understanding exactly what was so funny.

To the Clayton children the meal was a feast and their uncles were heroes. George would be content knowing that his family was fed. He would rather have been the provider, the hero, but, once again, he swallowed his pride, along with Mary's warm, delicious fried rabbit when he came home from work that night.

A few days later, George was given an opportunity to regain his position as the Clayton family provider when he brought home a snapping turtle he had found wandering along the sandy road. He knew that his children loved when they were allowed to help their mother clean and cook a big snapper. When Mary took the heart out of the turtle, it would amaze the children because it would beat for hours of its own accord. The turtle had to be parboiled until a thick, jelly-like substance floated to the top of the water in the kettle. Mary then easily removed the meat, rolled it in flour, and fried it in her large cast iron pan. The meat was tender and delicious. It had a similar taste to chicken. On occasion, Mary would make a scrumptious turtle soup.

Mary emphasized to her children that they were fortunate to have food at all, even if it was a bit odd or exotic. She liked to tell them how, up in the great north woods, a man could be lost for days or weeks with no food, and the only animal that was slow enough to catch, club, and cook would be a porcupine. It was a last resort meal for anyone, and they often referred to it as "lost man's food." The children did not think that they would enjoy a porcupine dinner. In fact, they crinkled their noses in disgust at the mere thought of eating such a thing.

Alta Fay was curious, though, and asked, "How would a man gut a porcupine without getting stabbed by the quills?"

"Well, he probably would get poked a few times, but when you're starvin' you get desperate. That's why they call it 'lost man's food,'" answered Mary.

Alta Fay was still not satisfied. "How could anyone get lost? I would never get lost nor eat a porcupine, either!"

Mary smiled and patiently replied, "Alta Fay, you have only lived in southern Michigan. It is not thick with trees like it is up north. People get lost real easy, and it happens more often than you think. They truly believe they're walking in a straight path toward a road or home, but they are really just walking in circles. It sounds silly, but I know it's true because I got lost one time when I was about twelve."

Alta's eyes grew large and round. She moved to the edge of her chair and listened intently to her mother's story.

"My family was mushroom picking up in the north woods one May, when I unknowingly wandered away from the group. Suddenly, I looked around and didn't see Big Grandma, Grandpa, Uncle Allen or Uncle Frank. The woods were real quiet in a creepy sort of way. Except for the birds, mosquitoes, and the wind whistling through the trees, I heard nothing. All I could think to do was run and yell, so that is what I did. In just a few minutes Grandpa Blanchard came running from over a knoll. He was yelling so that I would stop running, but my mind was so mixed up and my sense of direction so turned around that I ran directly away from him. He literally had to catch me! It's a good thing your ma was a slow runner," snickered Mary. Then she continued, "Some time later, Grandpa Blanchard said that when he topped that hill all he could see was me running in circles! I didn't believe him then, but I've heard too many similar stories to dispute it now."

Mary hoped that Alta Fay could understand how easily a person could get turned around. Fortunately, Mary was able to breathe a great sigh of relief when Alta Fay said, "O.K. I get it." Satisfied with the explanation, she skipped out of the kitchen.

    The irony of the story caused Mary to settle into her rocker and quietly ponder on this topic. The thickly forested north woods are a lot like the rest of the world. Hopelessly lost in its vastness, folks become scared and confused. In a state of panic the survival instinct is activated and they run. Their hope is to quickly find their way out of the skeleton-like branches and tangled brambles, without help. All too soon, though, they are overcome with exhaustion and, finally, defeat as they realize that they are right back where they started from. They gain nothing because they have only been running in circles. Unfortunately, many people run in circles their entire lives unless a father comes to rescue them. Gladly he will lead if they are willing to follow until all are safely home.

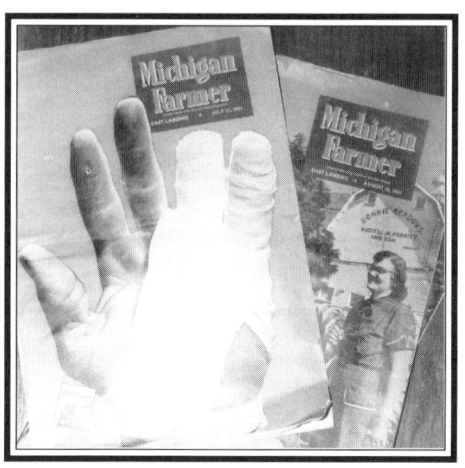

Chapter 4

The Good, the Bad, and the Chance to Succeed

GEORGE — IN HIS IMMATURE, INSECURE, and frustrated mindset — often blamed his badly dealt hand of life on God. He had to blame someone. On occasion he took his anger and pain out on Mary, and she would be in tears for days following his verbal abuse. He was always apologetic afterward and hated himself for losing his temper. He promised to not become so upset again, but it was a promise he never kept. The children knew what their daddy did wasn't right, and it broke their tiny hearts when Mamma had to endure the abuse as they hid helplessly. Unfortunately, George could not see what was truly important at the time, and, in his ignorance, he treated his family poorly and cursed God for his own failures.

Thankfully, after many years, George grew up. He no longer hurt Mary's feelings so often, and listened with compassion as she poured out her heart. With experience and hardship comes character, and George was developing a wealth of both during these challenging years. When a man has been brought to his knees enough times, and when he is as low as he can go, there is no place to look but up. Not many years passed before George looked up and eventually pleaded to the Lord for mercy and forgiveness. The contrition of this simple man, along with the positively changed lives of many others, gives further credibility to the notion that there were more blessings than misery during this trying period in America's history.

In truth, the Great Depression cannot justly be portrayed as only a negative time. Good came from it as well as extreme heartache for many families, including the Claytons. The Depression forced communities to work together for a common good, and families prayed together for what little they had been given. Many who had left it untouched for years read the Bible. Mary, like so many others who battled life through the Great Depression, believed the saying "That which does not kill you, shall make you stronger." In retrospect, this was accurate, but it had the taste of bitter medicine at the time.

It invigorated multitudes of disillusioned men and women when President Roosevelt began pulling the Americans out of a hole by their bootstraps. The society would eventually rebound under his strong leadership. By June 1933, his numerous relief programs were quickly implemented, and it was a lifeline for many families. These programs promised work for the men and a steady, decent income for their households, all the while maintaining their dignity. It was by no means a handout. Roads and buildings needed to be constructed, and if men were willing to work, President Roosevelt was willing to give them a chance to improve their lives. George was instilled with a good work ethic and took full advantage of this opportunity. Life for the poor family seemed to be changing for the better, and it had come none too soon. George fell asleep the night before his first day of work and happily thought, *Everything will be all right from now on.* He rolled onto his side, draped his strong arm over his wife, and drifted into a contented sleep.

Chapter 5

Early Summer 1933

IN THE MORNING, A COOL breeze whispered through the open window of the tiny, overcrowded bedroom and brushed gently across Phyllis's rosy cheek. The dawn sky was splashed with pale yellows, pinks, and blues. It looked like a freshly painted picture whose artist was a very young child. It was both simple and beautiful. The well-rested songbirds had awakened and were now chattering back and forth to one another, commenting on nature's grand introduction to the new day.

Phyllis's eyes fluttered and then opened. She had turned in early the previous night and received plenty of rest, so her entire body felt refreshed. She breathed in slowly and deeply the fresh morning air and smiled. It was the first day of summer vacation from the Demming's Lake Country School in Sand Creek, Michigan. School would not resume until after Labor Day. To everyone's delight, the summer's beginning promised to be warm and sunny, just as the Farmers' Almanac had predicted. Phyllis carefully rolled over and touched, as lightly as possible, the tip of her younger sister's nose with her forefinger.

When the effect of this proved fruitless in awakening her, Phyllis decided to change her strategy. She glanced down and discovered a single, dainty, down feather that had worked its way out of her pillow during the night; she repeated her teasing, using the delicately fine hairs. However, this time she carefully brushed the soft feather across her sister's lips. Alta Fay's eyes suddenly opened, and she sat up with a start, rubbing her lips in an attempt to cease the itching, irritating sensation of the feather. It was a dreadfully miserable feeling and Phyllis knew it. She triumphantly laughed and fell back on her pillow.

Just above a whisper, Phyllis asked, "Are you ever gonna get up, sleepy head?"

Alta Fay, without answering, began to playfully wrestle with her sister for a few moments until she tired, and then flopped back against her pillow laughing. She enjoyed wrestling and would, at times, become a bit too rough, but Alta Fay would never have done anything to intentionally hurt Phyllis.

"We get to go up to Grandma's this morning," Phil said excitedly.

Both girls sprang from their straw-filled mattress and dressed quickly. Any day they could spend at Grandma Blanchard's was a good day, even if work was involved. Both girls darted for the kitchen. The aroma of hot coffee and food lingered in the air. Mamma's slippers scraped across the hardwood floor and the handle that lifted the cast iron plate rattled as she added more kindling to the cook stove.

    Mary arose earlier than usual so that she could make the children a warm cup of tea and pack them a hearty lunch before they walked the mile to their grandparents' house. They would spend the day weeding onions in the mucky fields. Each row completely freed of weeds earned the worker five cents. Phyllis hated this work. In her eyes, the rows seemed to be a mile long. In addition, her fair complexion and fine, blond hair was no match for the hot summer sun. Many summer nights in the past she would return from the field looking like a beet red lobster. Her mama would rub vinegar, what little they could afford, into her red-hot skin to help ease the pain. Phyllis would lay in bed while Alta Fay applied cold rags to her arms and face. This helped her to sleep better. She learned quickly to keep her arms covered with a thin, long-sleeved light-colored cotton shirt, no matter the temperature. Mama made each of the girls a sunbonnet from saved scraps of material. This helped protect their ears, nose, and head from the scorching sun.

    There were endless rows of onions in Grandpa's field, and the smell of them seemed to remain in one's nostrils for a week or more after harvest. The entire family helped out when harvest time arrived. First, the onions were pulled and topped, and then they were carefully placed in Grandpa's wagon and brought to market. Before Grandpa Blanchard left, though, it was a yearly ritual that George would smile and say, "Looks like quite a load there, Inez," as he patted the immense wagonload of onions.

    Grandpa Blanchard would proudly reply, "Yep, even better than last year's, I do believe. I think we'll make out all right."

    George was always excited to know that the crop had been a plentiful one, because Grandpa Blanchard paid him for helping and also gave his family a share of the onions. These onions, along with a generous portion of Grandpa's garden vegetables, would help the family throughout the winter months. Big Grandma and Mamma spent days on end canning tomatoes, carrots, beans, corn, beets, squash, and pumpkins. Though, feeding an ever-growing family took quite a harvest. By winter's end there was scarcely anything left. Stretching a meal was an art that Depression mothers knew well.

Phyllis felt proud of all that her family had accomplished. Though very young, she was happy to be a part of it all, even if her focus and attention to that type of work was still that of a child. Neither Phyllis nor Alta Fay was given nearly the amount of responsibility that their older sisters, Barbara and Clare, were given, but they still had responsibilities all the same. Phyllis was happy to help out Grandma and Grandpa Blanchard, but if she had the choice she would remain home and care for the younger children. Phyllis's ideal scenario would be going to visit only when fieldwork needn't be done. At least some of her time at home, after chores, could be devoted to reading under a cool shade tree while the babies napped, or she could go adventuring with Alta Fay. Phyllis's dream-like scenario would never come to fruition until harvest time was over. The present moment demanded that rows of onions be weeded immediately.

Mamma jolted Phyllis and Alta Fay into action when she yelled out from the kitchen, "Those onions aren't gonna weed themselves! You two skeedaddle! See you this afternoon and listen to your grandma and grandpa. Hear now?"

As the girls stepped out onto the porch, they noticed a team and wagon making its way from the east toward their home. They stood still and shaded their eyes from the bright morning sun. When the person reached the end of the driveway, and the sun was no longer blinding the Claytons, they recognized that the wagon belonged to Mr. Taylor, the ragman.

Every six months this man would come to the neighborhood collecting old, worn-out scraps of material and clothing that were no longer of any use. He would pay his customers with a huge fish or two that he had caught in the Great Lakes. The Claytons would have enough fish for two or three meals, and the Ragman could earn his share by delivering the cloth scraps to the paper mill.

Mary wiped her hands on her apron, headed back into the house, and briskly walked upstairs. The morning was quickly warming, and, with each step, beads of sweat were forming on Mary's forehead. When a single drop of perspiration traveled a crooked path down her back, it felt as if a creepy spider were crawling across it. Mary's cotton dress stuck uncomfortably to the dampness. In a few minutes, she would open the second story window, breathe in fresh, cool air, then begin throwing the rags out into the Ragman's wagon, which was stopped directly below, just inches from the side of the house.

Barbara and Clare followed their mother upstairs in order to help her fetch the rags. Phyllis and Alta Fay stayed out of the way. Too many hands in the small upstairs room would only shorten fuses. Instead these two girls stared into the long, ice-filled box that stretched across the back of the ragman's wagon. Neither girl knew what kind of fish were laying in this ice, but they sure had huge, bulging eyes!

"Got some good fish there, girls," commented the ragman as he busily rearranged several objects in the wagon's bed in order to make room for the rags.

"They look kinda spooky to me, Mr. Taylor," said Phyllis candidly.

"Yeah, those are some ugly eyes. What do you think Ms. Alta Fay?" he asked, glancing her way.

"Oh, I don't know. They're a bit smelly, but I sure like the way Ma cooks 'em up," commented Alta Fay.

Changing the subject, Mr. Taylor said, "You two look as if you've each grown six inches since I last saw you." Both girls blushed and giggled as they accepted Mr. Taylor's compliments.

Thunk! went the first of the rags. The Ragman turned his attention to the upper story window and warned Mary, "You be careful. I don't want you throwing yourself out that window!"

"I'm fine. Thanks. I haven't many more to toss out," replied Mary.

In a short time all the rags had been thrown into the wagon, the window was closed, and Barbara and Clare again appeared on the porch. Politely they said good morning to Mr. Taylor. Phyllis and Alta Fay were still gawking at the huge, slimy, lifeless fish.

Mary followed Barbara and Clare out onto the porch and spoke with the ragman. "Would you like a cup of coffee?" asked Mary, in her sweet, hospitable way.

"Thank you, kindly, Mrs. Clayton. But this is the first stop of the morning, and I really need to be getting back to the mill 'fore noon," replied Mr. Taylor.

Mary noticed her two younger girls staring and scolded them. "You just help get the fish out and into the house instead of gawking!"

The Ragman handed each of the girls a fish and they quickly carried them into the house, flopped them onto the table, and hurried back out. It wasn't often they had company.

Finished with the present work and ready to be on his way, the ragman climbed back onto his wagon.

"You have a good day. It looks like it'll be a warm one," said Mary.

The girls waved from the bottom step of the porch. Mr. Taylor grasped the brim of his hat with his index finger and thumb and tipped it as he nodded his farewell to the ladies. He clucked to the horses, snapped the reigns, and the team started off, leaving a dusty wake.

Mary, for the second time, bade her children "goodbye" and sent them on their way. She was relieved that Mr. Taylor had not accepted her invitation and that it didn't take long to barter, because her tooth was aching terribly. She was not sure if she could even take the extra time to fix the fish for tonight's supper. Poor man's stew would be quicker and easier. She felt there was no choice but to ask George, when he returned from work, if he would take care of the fish.

The older girls set out toward their grandparents' farm and the two younger ones, Phyllis and Alta Fay, straggled along behind. They kicked up dust, picked spring wildflowers, popped the heads off of dandelion weeds, and chased each other. When Alta Fay discovered an old can along the way, they played a great game of Kick the Can until the Blanchard farm came into view. The result of their dawdling was that they were twenty minutes late to Grandma and Grandpa's. Fortunately for these girls, their grandparents were patient people who understood the behaviors of children.

"Good morning, young ladies," Grandma said. She hugged and kissed each of her grandchildren as they entered her warm, comfortable kitchen. The white, paint chipped screen door shut with a dull thud. Phyllis shot a glance toward the floor, knowing well what had happened. It had not slammed, as usual, because the old calico cat was in its way. It let out a short yowl and streaked for cover behind the warm cook stove. This was not an uncommon occurrence, and Grandma paid little attention to it. Without looking back, Grandma intuitively assured the exasperated girls with a tisk and brush of her hand. "The cat will be fine. Come and eat some breakfast before it gets cold."

Phyllis was unsure. She knelt down next to the wall and stretched her arm carefully into the opening until her fingers reached the cat's head. In the shadows behind the stove she could faintly see the end of its long tail flicking methodically back and forth, back and forth. If it is possible that a tail can look angry, this tail did. Phyllis scratched the cat's head and under its soft chin. The cat pointed his nose toward the sky, soon forgetting that it had been injured only minutes ago. Its slanted eyes slowly closed, relishing in this gentle human's attention. Quietly at first, then increasing in volume, Phyllis could hear the steady, content purring of the cat. She was now sure that he would be all right, and that satisfied her anxiety.

After washing up at the sink in a tin wash basin that was filled to the brim with luke-warm, cloudy water, Phyllis and Alta Fay rushed to the table and fairly gobbled down the thin, golden pancakes Grandma had made for them. At home their mother made pancakes on the occasional weekend. This was a feast for them. When their bellies were full, they politely cleared the table and set the dishes in the old, white porcelain sink. Wiping their syrupy mouths on the sleeves of their dresses, they headed for the door. Grandma carefully handed Phyllis the lunch basket and followed them out onto the porch. She waved goodbye as her grandkids dashed down the steps. While they were still within earshot, Grandma yelled, "Slow down, you two! Your breakfast ain't even hit your stomach, and you're off like a bear's on your heals!"

Phyllis and Alta Fay glanced back and laughed. Not missing a step, they waved over their shoulders and behind their backs to their overly protective grandma.

The onion field was not far from the Blanchard's house, and it would have been fine if the children came back to eat their lunch. However, taking Grandma's homemade picnic basket full of their mamma's goodies was a treat, and it made the children feel more grown up. Grandma knew this and slowly walked down around noonday to the soft green edge of the mucky field. She gracefully bowed as she asked permission to dine with the children.

"Aw, you don't need to ask us, Grandma!" exclaimed Alta Fay, running to Grandma and throwing her arms around her big, round body.

Grandma smiled. "I know I needn't ask, but you girls are growing up so quickly I thought it was the proper and polite thing to do."

Playing along, Phyllis proudly stated, "Permission granted."

Grandma proceeded to lay a huge blanket on the thick green grass and set up for lunch. This was a wonderful treat for them. Big Grandma, as her grandchildren called her, told wonderfully beautiful tales. They became queens and princesses attending gala parties with lots of delicious food. Rested and content, they began to get dreamy and nodded off during her stories. It was a refreshing short escape before returning to reality and the onion field. Big Grandma rubbed their backs and smoothed their fine hair as they relaxed. How she dearly loved her grandchildren. However, she worried incessantly, as grandmothers (and mothers) do, about something dreadful happening to one of them. She knew that the likelihood of such an occurrence was small, yet it haunted her thoughts, lurking in the shadows of the uncertainty of life. She hoped she would never have to deal with such a tragedy, because she wasn't sure that she was mentally or physically capable of handling it.

"Trust in the Lord," Big Grandma repeated to herself. Like cobwebs hanging from the corner of a dusty, overlooked doorway, Grandma mentally brushed the negative thoughts out of her mind. Her grandchildren would be all right. She must believe that or go crazy with worry.

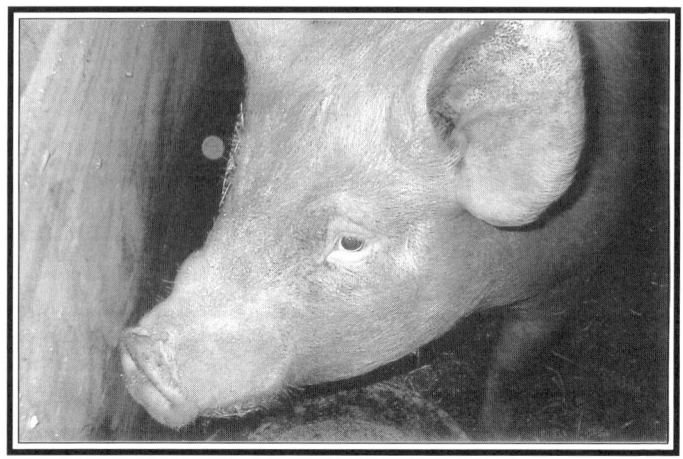

Chapter 6

Judy

By early afternoon, Phyllis became bored. It was much too long of a time span for a seven year old. She pulled slowly at the ugly weeds. The motion was almost mechanical; she didn't need to even think about the process because it had become as natural as breathing. Her idle mind began to wander, and she thought back to the cat incident earlier that morning.

Phyllis always thought it was funny that the cat had no name. It was referred to only as "Cat." She realized farmers live hard, demanding lives, and that the births and demise of farm animals are a part of their every day lives. Phyllis reckoned that it made sense that if farmers were to name all of their animals, it would make it more difficult when something happened to them. Cows, pigs, and chickens were butchered; horses had to be put down because of a broken leg or colic, and cats and dogs were accidentally shot, hit by cars, or killed by large predators lurking in the woods. An animal's life usually ends in some sort of violent way. That is nature.

Phyllis went back in her mind a few years. She recalled how she wished she had never named the family's pig. She should have called it Pig, like grandma called the cat, Cat. That may have lessened the impact on her when she learned of the pig's demise.

ONE SPRING MORNING, George brought home a pig he had bartered from a neighbor. This pig was massive and was the most intriguing creature Phyllis had ever seen. Every day she would toss corn, potato peelings, and table scraps (of which there were very few) over the wood slab fence and into the pen. Daddy made sure that the children were careful around this animal. An old sow could get ornery and should not be trusted. For the most part, the children obeyed their father. Phyllis named this pig "Judy." All the children thought the pig was grand, and they referred to it by the name Judy, at Phyllis's request. Unlike her sisters and brothers, Phyllis quickly developed a special place in her heart for this calf-sized sow. On hot summer days she watched its huge mass as it lay in the cool muck, flies hovering and alighting on its snout and body. Its leathery skin would twitch periodically in response to the irritating feeling of the crawling, buzzing creatures. Sometimes the old sow lay so still that Phyllis had to stare at its pinkish brown stomach until she saw it slowly rise and fall, rise and fall, to make sure that it was still alive.

Phyllis thought Judy should rightly have been named "The Intimidator," because all of the children were frightened of her. Phyllis never entered the pen when the pig was there, but the minute Judy was put out into another section of the yard, Phyllis and the other children scrambled to play inside her house, which their papa had built into the side of a hill. The children had respected Judy and their father's wish to be wary of this animal at all times.

It had been a great summer having Judy around the yard, but, all too soon, Labor Day rolled around and country school was in session again. Phyllis loved school and did well in her studies. Although schoolwork kept her busy, she always found time to spend with Judy. Mamma shook her head as she observed her young daughter talking to the pig. "It's gonna break her heart to have to butcher the pig, but we've warned her many times," she would tell George.

"She'll just have to learn, Mary. She's got to grow up sometime. She will be all right," George would reply, though, not sounding real confident.

One warm autumn day, after school, Phyllis gently laid her book and tablet onto the soft green grass, took off the beautiful red sweater her mamma had knitted for her, and carefully hung it on the old fence post near Judy's pen. She stood on the top edge of the lowest pine board and peered inside.

"Hello there, Judy," Phyllis said sweetly. "How's my old gal?" she asked. The big old sow responded with a series of noisy grunts.

"You look hungry, Judy," observed Phyllis, so she sprinted into the house to collect all of the scraps her mamma had saved throughout the day. On her way back to the pen Phyllis smiled as she imagined Judy eagerly awaiting her wonderful gift of corncobs, potato and apple peelings, and the rind from a watermelon. However, when she arrived at the pen her smile faded. She noticed immediately that her sweater was gone. Had one of the other children taken it as a joke? Phyllis, for the life of her, could not figure out what had happened to it. Giving up speculation, she peered into Judy's pen. Her hand instantly loosened its grip on the pail handle and the bucket of middling dropped to the ground with a thud, spilling the contents everywhere. Phyllis was horrified. That pig had actually eaten it!

"You nasty, no-good fat pig! How dare you, Judy!" Phyllis began to cry.

Alta Fay heard her sister yelling and ran to the crime scene as fast as her legs could carry her. Out of breath, Alta Fay questioned, "What's up, Phil? Why ya' cryin'?"

"Th-Th-The…Ju-Judy ate my sweater," Phyllis stammered, wiping her eyes and pointing into the muddy pen. Several small red pieces could be seen scattered throughout the muck. Though Phyllis was startled and angry, she was much more disappointed in the animal's apparent betrayal.

"Well, I ought to take a stick to her, Phil," said Alta Fay as she searched around for the desired object.

"No," said Phil. "She doesn't know any better." Yes, Judy was of mammoth proportions and intimidated anyone who came near her, yet Phyllis assumed she had developed a rapport with this peculiar old sow. "I just never thought a pig would eat a piece of clothing," Phyllis said in confusion.

"I didn't think it would either. Stupid pig," Alta Fay insulted Judy, thinking she was sticking up for her sister. Phyllis didn't mind when she called Judy bad names out of anger, but she immediately came to Judy's defense when someone else did. "She's not stupid; she's just a…just a…a pig," replied Phyllis. For a moment they stared at each other in silence. Then, both girls began laughing uncontrollably. Phyllis's simple, candid observation had been a momentary tension breaker.

Finally, the girls calmed down and began walking back to the house, in a sober manner. Remembering again what had just taken place, Phyllis began to cry softly. It had been her only sweater, and it had taken so much of her mother's valuable time to make. Alta Fay placed her arm around her sister. She was hurting because Phyllis was hurting.

Mama, at first, acted angry as Phyllis sobbed through the story, but she calmly stated, "Those things happen, Phil. You've learned a lesson, and just make sure it doesn't happen again."

"I'm so sorry, Mamma," Phyllis cried, hugging her mother. Without another word Mary silently accepted the apology, rested her cheek on the top of Phyllis's head and hugged her tightly.

Later that night Phyllis and Alta Fay could hear Mamma re-telling the story to daddy. He laughed and then Mamma began to giggle. It was a sweet, sweet sound in their ears.

In October, the weather began to change. The air was colder, and gray lines of smoke snaked skyward from the neighbors' chimneys in the valley. Some nights there would be such hard frosts that when Phyllis awoke in the morning she could not see out of her window. Crystals covered it in a thick, frozen layer. The ground was the same. It would take the warm morning sun only a few hours to make the frost disappear. The children walked the mile and a half to school at a brisk pace in order to keep warm. The Clayton children were always eager to please their teacher. If they arrived early, each child would carry an armload of firewood inside and stack it neatly in the back corner, behind the desks, to help out the old school teacher. She was a strict but fair lady, and she always thanked the children for their thoughtfulness. Besides teaching the three R's to a large group of children with disparate academic abilities, it was also the teacher's job to periodically feed firewood to the hungry wood stove that stood proudly in the center of the large room.

Phyllis thought it was nice to be the first to arrive because she liked to pick a school desk nearest the stove. Alta Fay was thin and became cold very easily, so Phyllis always made sure to save her a choice seat as well.

By early November the trees were bare and the wind whipped with an angry fury. The children's noses were red, and they were constantly snuffling. One afternoon, when Phyllis returned from school, she noticed that Judy was gone. She wondered if she had gotten loose some time during the day, as was common for the old sow to do. In confusion, Phyllis wandered to the house. When she opened the back door, the aroma of a delicious dinner rushed out and into her face. Phyllis suddenly realized how hungry she was. However, something did not appear quite right. It was not often that dinner, like the one she now smelled, carried such an amazing aroma. Maybe Thanksgiving, Christmas, Easter, or a once-in-a-while Sunday dinner would have this scent. But, an ordinary, after school dinner never smelled so delicious. However, instead of bringing her joy, this left Phyllis with an uneasy, unsettling feeling deep inside her. As she entered the kitchen and was about to ask her mamma if she knew the whereabouts of Judy, the dark thought that had gradually seeped into her mind was now unleashed like a violent storm. They had butchered her pig!

Judy's watermelon of a head lay in halves on a cracked China platter in the middle of the dining room table. Mamma sat, expertly using a razor on its ears and snout. The sight was too much for Phyllis. Her legs became weak, but she managed to wobble into the children's bedroom before falling on her knees and breaking down in tears. It hurt so badly that she didn't think her crying would ever end.

Meanwhile, Mary continued the messy chore. She removed the eyes and teeth and washed the skull until the two halves were white like ivory. Finally, in her huge pot, she boiled the meat off the bone, ground it, and added sage, along with several other spices in order to make headcheese. Usually this tasted mighty good, but the thought of eating it at the moment made Phyllis develop a burning, choking lump in her throat as though she may, at any second, vomit.

It was the usual practice that Mamma took the fat from the pig and rendered it out to use during the winter months. Of course, anyone who has ever lived on a farm knows that. The leftovers from the fat baking in the oven are called cracklings, and Mamma would break it up and sprinkle it on the corn bread. It tasted wonderful.

It was also common practice that, whenever a pig was butchered, Phyllis and her siblings would draw straws to see who got to eat the pig's tail. Mama would place it in the oven and roast it until the outside was a dark brown. The taste was that of bacon or roast pork, something that any hungry child would desire. However, Phyllis declined to participate on this occasion.

Each time a pig is slaughtered, like today, the children know that their mamma will make them pork liver for supper. This dinner was a special treat for everyone but Phyllis. Her stomach flip-flopped with anxiety at the thought of eating her poor old sow Judy.

Once Mamma finished the messy job, she washed and dried her hands on her apron and entered the room where Phyllis quietly lay. Mary softly touched her daughter on the shoulder. Phyllis turned over and sat up. Her eyes were swollen and red from crying. Mamma drew her tenderhearted daughter close to her bosom.

She softly explained, "Phil, I am sorry that you had grown so attached to the pig, but you know how we are struggling and the family's needs come first. Daddy brought the old sow home with the intent of butchering it this fall. He did not hide that from you."

Phyllis could not dispute this truth, though it did not stop the tears. She learned, for a second time, from this situation, that the farmer's life is a tough one, and she vowed never to allow herself to become so attached to the livestock again.

Oil Painting by Amber Ellis

Chapter 7

Grandpa's Surprise

"PHYLLIS? I'VE BEEN CALLING TO you for the last ten minutes," complained Alta Fay. "You finished your row and have been sittin' there like you're in a trance or something. Are you feelin' O.K.?" Alta Fay's voice sounded concerned as she retrieved Phyllis from her reveries of Judy and brought her back to the onion field.

"Yes, I was just daydreaming I guess. Is it time to head for home?" Phyllis questioned.

"Yeah, Barbara and Clare have some more to do, but Grandma said we could go and play," replied Alta Fay, with a grin.

The girls ran to the house and up the porch steps two at a time. This time Phyllis made sure the cat wasn't coming in when the screen door slammed shut.

"For Goodness sakes, you two sure are in a hurry to be off," chuckled grandma as she opened her worn out change purse. She firmly pressed two nickels into each of the girls' hands, and then squeezed their fingers tightly shut around the coins.

"Now, you take care not to lose your earnings. Keep it in a safe place." Grandma's look was kind yet stern because money was so scarce. Both girls gave their grandma a serious look directly into her wise, old eyes to assure her that the money would indeed be safe with them. Satisfied that the girls would act responsibly with their newly found fortune, Grandma continued her safety warnings while handing them each a loaf of bread. It is a God-given right for grandmas to perform this ritual with grandchildren.

Though the children rarely saw a car, Grandma ordered the girls to "watch out for cars and wagons and head straight home!" She kissed each of their cheeks and sent them away carrying the loaves of freshly baked bread under their arms. "Don't smash the bread now, you hear? It's fresh from the oven!" grandma warned. "Tell your mamma hello for me and let me know if that tooth of hers is still causin' her fits. I'll be more than glad to get old Mattie Squires to come over with her pliers and she'll take care of it," Grandma said.

"O.K., Grams," the girls yelled over their shoulders. Grandma wondered, as she turned to go back into the house, if the bread would survive the trip home without being crushed. As she went back through the doorway the screen thudded behind her, pinching the cat again. Knowing instantly what kept the screen from banging shut, she shook her head back

Grandpa and the Farmer's Almanac

and forth, rolled her eyes, and went back to her sink of dishes.

About half way home the girls spotted a team of horses coming toward them. There was no mistaking who it could be. It was Grandpa Blanchard, coming from town. They loved this stout, friendly grandpa. Whether it is Sunday dinner or bringing his team of horses and cultivator down to work some land, the children's eyes sparkled with love and admiration upon seeing their favorite grandpa. That is why, at harvest time each year, going to market with the load of onions always made Phyllis sad. Grandpa allowed no one to ride with him, but Phyllis would surely have jumped at the opportunity. He was kind and generous and always had an exciting story to share. He was a small man with very little hair, and he looked awkward when he stood next to Grandma Blanchard, who was tall and heavy.

Alta Fay was the first to notice that Grandpa Blanchard had a burlap bundle resting in his lap. *What could he be bringing from town?* both girls wondered to themselves. They assumed that Grandma had sent him for some material goods from Leonard's General Store. Packages of any sort were exciting to both the receiver and the onlooker.

In a few short minutes the wagon was stopped alongside two of Grandpa's beautiful grandkids. "Whoa," he yelled to the team. They obeyed instantly. They were two of the most admirable horses in the county. They were shires, the most gentle of all horses. These mares appeared quite similar in color — chestnut and brown with feathered white socks, and a distinct white line ran from their forelocks to their muzzles. They were a proud duo and were the center of attention everywhere they went.

Alta Fay, standing on tiptoe, brushed the flank of one with her left hand as she shielded the afternoon sun from her eyes with her right. The bundle on their grandpa's lap jerked about, and both Alta Fay's and Phyllis's eyes instantly grew as large and round as saucers. Cautiously, they edged closer to their grandpa. A tiny, brownish-red nose poked out of the gunny sack and grandpa was obliged to take the remainder of the cloth prison off.

"It's a baby deer!" cried Phyllis as she tried to climb up the side of the wagon, Alta Fay on her heels. Its white spots were bright and round. Every feature of this beautiful creature was in miniature form. It seemed so fragile and frightened. Phyllis noticed that Grandpa kept a tight hold on its legs because fawns' legs are strong and can seriously injure someone if they are caught off guard. Alta Fay was totally absorbed in the situation. Leaning on Phyllis she asked, "Where'd you get it, Grandpa? Huh?"

"Some poachers killed the mother deer and the fawn was orphaned, I'm guessin,'" was Grandpa's experienced reply. "I noticed it lying in the high grass along the edge of the road on my way from town." His wagon sat high off the ground, and he had a much better view than the average person traveling on foot or by car. Grandpa hunted deer in season, but his heart melted as he held this tiny animal. It was so helpless, and he wanted to see it live.

"Are you two done with your weeding already?" Grandpa asked.

Neither of the girls' eyes left the fawn, and, for a moment, Grandpa wasn't sure if they had heard him. Phyllis finally looked at Grandpa and said, "Yeah, Grandma said we could go home and play."

"Well, I'd better not hold you two up then. I'll see you later," Grandpa said.

It would be difficult for the girls to continue their journey home, knowing Grandpa was heading back with the fawn. Grandpa sensed the girls' reluctance to leave, but insisted, "You take your ma's bread to her before you come running back, you hear?"

Those were the words they secretly desired to hear. Grandpa was inviting them to come back later! No way would they miss this chance if they could help it.

Hesitantly, but obediently, Phyllis and Alta Fay turned toward home. Moments later they began running like racehorses the entire way. Each girl wanted to be the first to tell Mamma the surprise news.

Chapter 8

Old Mattie Squires

MARY WAS CHANGING THE BABY'S soiled diapers as the excited girls burst through the front door, both attempting to talk at once. Five-year-old Jonathon was attempting to console an agitated Michael, and in the kitchen, a pot of poor man's soup was bubbling furiously on the stove. Mary's nerves were frayed, and she felt on the brink of collapsing. Sensing something was wrong, the girls abruptly stopped talking and stood still. In their excitement, they had not realized how stressful things were for their mamma at that moment. In response, Phyllis immediately searched out the toddler that was wailing, and Alta Fay headed straight for the kitchen to stir the soup. A few minutes later Mary appeared in the kitchen, washed her hands, and then plunked heavily onto a chair at the table. Phyllis followed, carrying her puffy, red-eyed little brother. Their mamma looked exhausted and in pain.

Sucking in a deep breath of air, Mamma demanded, "Now, what was making you two girls act like a couple of monkey-baboons when you came in the house?"

Again, both girls began to jabber at once.

"Whoa, one at a time," requested Mamma, holding her hand up in a halting manner.

Alta Fay graciously conceded and became silent. Phyllis, being the older of the two, was the one to rightfully lead the explanation. Mary tried to sound excited, but the pain would not let her. Though their excitement and interest was piqued, Alta Fay changed the subject. She had remembered the bread, and proudly handed the freshly baked loaves to Mamma. She smiled and said, "Oh, thank you. That Big Grandma sure is a good one. This will be wonderful with our soup." Mamma didn't have many of the supplies she needed to bake, like Big Grandma, as funds for the necessary ingredients were scarce. Daddy was a proud man and did not like to receive "handouts," as he referred to help that was given by friends and neighbors. It was especially degrading to accept necessities from his in-laws. He felt as if he was not capable of supporting his wife, their daughter, and his children, their grandchildren.

"We'll tell Daddy that I scraped up enough ingredients to make these here two loaves, O.K.?" Mamma winked. She didn't have that streak of pride when it came to feeding her children. A mamma has to think about what is best for her children and not her ego, and this was one of those times.

She was even more thankful for her mother's generosity because her tooth had been giving her such fits that she was unable to do any baking, even if it were just hardtack. Mary was silently thankful that her own mamma still kept an eye on her. It helped her to feel taken care of instead of her always taking care of everyone else, and she needed care now. George did what he could, when he could. But often it was just Mary and the children, battling through life. Mary silently wished, *Oh, George. How I need you to be home with me and the kids.*

Daddy had a steady job working on the roads for one of President Roosevelt's Federal Emergency Relief Administration Programs, and wouldn't be home until well after dark. As much as she dreaded the thought of taking George from a paying job, Mary wasn't sure how much more she could endure without some help.

The dinner was scrumptious and filling for the children, but Mamma was having a difficult time trying to eat with her aching tooth.

The girls knew that Mamma was in much more pain than she was expressing. Mary did not take care of her teeth as a child. It was not a priority for a struggling family. Many of her teeth had decayed to the point of needing to be extracted, but, again, there was no money. Mamma was the type that, even if the money were available, she would rather have spent it on George and the children's needs. Her endearing unselfish quality caused her extensive grief. At this point, with swelling and infection present, delay could cost her her life if not taken care of promptly. One had only to look into Mamma's eyes to see her agony. Often, as she sat at the table that afternoon, she would squeeze her eyes shut and hold her hand against her red, feverish cheek. Though the summer day was warm, Mamma was shivering.

As much as they wanted to see the fawn, the girls knew one of them must run to tell Big Grandma that Mamma's tooth was becoming unbearably painful for her. Alta Fay agreed to go, and Phyllis stayed behind to help with the children and the cleaning up of dinner. Mamma hugged her gratefully and cried a little. Phyllis cradled her and whispered, "I know it hurts, Mamma. Alta Fay just took off for Big Grandma's. She'll get Ms. Squires here as soon as she can." It hurt to see Mamma so fragile, but Phyllis did not feel that Mamma was weak or childish. She was so very strong and could endure so much. Phyllis had tears rolling down her cheeks in empathy toward her mama. *I will hold her and rub her back as long as she needs,* vowed Phyllis to herself. For some time, the two sat quietly holding each other. The afternoon dragged on, warm and quiet. The happenings of this world rolled on and on like tumbleweed in a steady breeze, never stopping to notice sicknesses or wellness, dying or living. It just rolled along indifferently.

Finally, Mamma broke the silence. She lifted herself off of Phyllis's lap, wiped her eyes and nose, and then encouraged her thoughtful daughter. "You go on now. I'll be all right. I'd really like to have the kitchen cleaned up and a plate ready for your dad when he gets home. He's so hungry after such a long day." Phyllis reluctantly did as her mother requested. It seemed to help Mary to rest and cry for a short time. The role reversal showed her how grown up and caring Phyllis was, though she was not surprised. She could depend on her children as they depended on her. It was a comforting feeling.

About an hour had passed when, from the kitchen, Phyllis heard the bells on the shires approaching. She rushed to the doorway. Peering out, she could see Barbara, Clare, Alta Fay, Big Grandma, and Grandpa Blanchard, along with Old Mattie Squires and her pliers. That was a name they called her around town because she always carried a pair of pliers with her. She believed it was the universal tool. "Pliers can fix just about anything," Old Lady Squires would brag. Lord knows what she would have done if she had lived to see the invention of duct tape!

"They're comin', Mamma!" Phyllis shouted back into the house.

Mama mumbled something but Phyllis couldn't understand her.

She ran out to the wagon, raising a cloud of dust that Grandma tried to wave away, and fairly dragged the rescuers into where her mamma was sitting.

"Hold on there, Phil. We're a comin' fast as these old tired bodies can, girl," Big Grandma said.

After stepping off of the wagon, Grandpa Blanchard reached up and took Mattie's doctoring bag in one hand and offered to help her down with the other. Mattie blushed. She was not used to men folk raising such a fuss over her. Old Mattie would never have admitted it, but she enjoyed the attention.

Grandma didn't mind that Grandpa had shown his politeness toward Mattie; she could get in and out of a wagon without the aid of anyone. Holding onto the side of the wagon with one hand, Big Grandma could kick both legs to the side, hurtle herself over and lightly land on the ground, still on her two feet. Grandpa helped Big Grandma down from the wagon once in a while, like on Sunday, but he didn't make much over her in public. She was fiercely independent, and she would have taken offense to an overabundance of this type of gesture. Grandpa admired that in her. Big Grandma was confident and strong. She made a good wife and a good friend.

Though it hurt too much to smile, Mamma was never so happy to see Old Mattie in all her life. She tried to act as if everyone was making too much out of her toothache. It embarrassed her to be the center of attention over a dental problem. Getting up to brew a pot of coffee, Mary attempted to be the jovial hostess. Grandma Blanchard stopped her.

"You stay right there in that chair, Mary," ordered her mother. "We will take care of things."

Mary did as she was told and was silently relieved.

Many folks in the valley could not afford to go to a dentist, so they relied on this old spinster to care for their emergency dental needs. In exchange, the patient's family would send her home with a chicken or some freshly baked goods as payment for her services.

Old Mattie washed her hands and dried them on Mamma's kitchen towel. "Well, what we got here, Mary?" she asked, not expecting an answer. "Looks like you could've used me a couple a days ago by the looks of that there inflamed cheek!" Old Mattie was a direct and to-the-point person. She wasn't one to hold back on account of etiquette. She approached Mamma and pried her mouth open, squinting and bobbing her head like a chicken, trying to get the best view of the bad tooth. "Yep, there it is, rotten as an October tomato still sittin' in the garden," commented Old Mattie as she reached for her pliers. The rest of the spectators were squinting and crinkling their noses and twisting their mouths into contorted shapes of pain. Standing back, Phyllis almost laughed aloud at the family's gawking. It would have made a funny photograph.

Grandma turned to her grandchildren and began giving a long list of orders. "You kids go on out and play a while. Your mamma doesn't need an audience. Stay in the yard and watch the little ones so they don't go wandering off into the woods."

Phyllis wondered how one person could hold all of those orders in their head and spit them out in a moment's notice like they were on the end of her tongue, all the time just aching to come out. She released them all in one breath. Grandma was truly amazing.

Without pondering that thought anymore, Phyllis instantly sprang into action. She didn't say a word, but quickly gathered the little ones and took them outside to play. The children sat in a small circle on the soft grass, and Alta Fay told them about the fawn that Grandpa Blanchard brought home. They hung on her every word and could hardly wait to see the beautiful creature for themselves. Phyllis admiringly smiled at Alta Fay and said, "You sure can tell a good story. You should write some of them down. I bet you could even be a writer when you grow up."

Alta Fay smiled modestly and replied, "I've been thinkin' about being a writer. I might even be famous and have lots of money that I could give to Mamma and Daddy."

The group sat quietly for a moment, dreaming Alta Fay's dream, when the stillness of the early evening was suddenly pierced with Mamma's cries of pain. It was dreadful for Phyllis to listen to, and the young children began to cry, knowing something was hurting their Mamma. Alta Fay attempted to continue her stories, hoping to capture the children's attention. It was not working the way she had intended. In a flash, the children sprang to their feet and began toddling toward the house, trying to get to their mamma. It took all of the girls' strength to corral them in. It hurt Phyllis and Alta Fay to have to do this, but they knew it must be done. Mamma would want it that way.

Suddenly, all was quiet. In the silence, the children stopped crying and attempting to break free from their sisters. Everyone stood as still as statues. Only their eyes darted back and forth, from one sibling to another. Clare walked out onto the porch, down the steps and across the yard in long strides. Smiling, she reported that Mamma's tooth was out and that everything would be fine. As if that were their cue, the children began running toward the house. They needed to see for themselves that their mamma was fine. Secondhand information just would not do to relieve their anxiety.

Mamma was sitting in the kitchen chair holding an ice filled cloth against her cheek. Just having the tooth out had eased her pain considerably. Mattie placed a peroxide soaked cotton ball into the gaping hole in Mamma's gum. "This is to help fight the infection," explained Mattie to the children.

Mamma thanked her, and Grandma offered Mattie a cup of coffee before they left. Mattie would go back to her home with a loaf of Grandma's bread and some delicious cinnamon rolls. Old Mattie Squires was thoroughly satisfied with the payment. Her smile told it all.

Observing all that was happening, Phyllis promised herself that she would make a special May basket, even though it was the middle of summer, fill it with all sorts of pretty flowers, and hang it on Old Mattie's door. It would be her way of expressing her gratitude for Miss Squires's service to her mother.

"I sincerely appreciate the baked goods, Mrs. Blanchard," said Old Mattie. "You know, I'd do it for nothin'," she added humbly.

"I know you would, Mattie, but we wouldn't hear of not giving you something for your indispensable service," Big Grandma explained. Mattie smiled as modestly as she could.

Then, turning to Mary and shaking her finger, Old Mattie ordered, "Now you keep that cleaned out, you hear?"

"Yes, Ma'am," said Mamma weakly, but relieved.

Grandpa and Grandma kissed Mamma and told Phyllis and the other girls to help get the little ones ready for bed. Before they went out into the cool dusk, Grandma kissed her girls and said, "I'll see you in the morning. I can hear those weeds a growin' as we speak!" With a wave and a smile Big Grandma was gone.

It was dark by the time the shires pulled up to Mattie's front gate. Grandpa helped the old lady down once again and he and Grandma both thanked her. "Goodnight, Mattie," the Blanchards called back as Grandpa hoisted himself back onto the wagon seat. He waved and then clucked for the shires to move on. It had been a very long day for the elderly couple.

With that ordeal over, the family could once again get on with their lives. The children could now focus attention again on the little fawn that Grandpa Blanchard had brought back to his farm. They were all anxious to see it. As soon as Mamma was feeling up to it and had the time, they would all take the trip up to Big Grandma's. Meanwhile, Phyllis and Alta Fay continued to run there every morning to weed onions and play.

Chapter 9

Dottie

THE JOB OF PULLING WEEDS in the onion field was not so bothersome now that there was a bright-eyed, beautiful fawn to cuddle and play with at Big Grandma's house.

"I think your little deer is a doe," commented Grandpa as the girls walked into the barn one morning.

Alta Fay began to think about the information Grandpa had just given them. Her index finger methodically tapped her chin. Suddenly, her eyes grew wide with revelation, and she confidently declared that she had an idea for the fawn's name. "I think we should call it Dottie because of all the tiny spots on her back," said Alta Fay, smiling proudly.

Phyllis agreed that the name was fitting for their brown and white-spotted bundle of joy. However, Phyllis tried to silently distance herself. In the back of her mind, she thought of pets or farm animals and how she had vowed never to name one again because of their inevitably violent demise. She could not bear to let Alta Fay know what she was thinking because it would have made her too sad.

Each morning, like clockwork, the girls arrived early to watch Grandpa feed the fawn. He took an empty, quart-sized pop bottle, filled it with fresh cow's milk, attached a makeshift nipple to the end, and fed it to Dottie like a baby. She would suck so hard that the nipple would stretch and almost snap off the end if Grandpa wasn't careful to keep an eye on it. The girls giggled at its eagerness to drink.

"Grandpa," asked Alta Fay, "did you ever see a fawn being born?"

"No, can't say as I have, Alta. But I've seen 'em when they are just a few minutes to a few hours old, standing on their oversized gangly legs. They wobble all over trying to get the hang of walking, then running. They sure are cute creatures."

"Why don't we see more fawns around, Grandpa?" Alta Fay continued her questioning.

"Well, a lot of times the mamma hides them real good. She has to, you know. There are always predators out there like coyotes and bobcats that can take down a tiny fawn real easily for a meal. That's what happens to some of them, and others are orphaned, like Dottie. But many still grow up and eventually become does and bucks," Grandpa replied as best he could.

"I don't like those coyotes and bobcats chasing baby deer, Grandpa," said Alta in a solemn voice.

"Well, that's nature. The mamma deer will kick at the predator and try to lure it away from her baby. She will do all she can to try and save its life, but sometimes there is nothing she can do. The predator will pounce on the fawn and within seconds it's too late for anything to be done about it. The mamma stays in the area after the death of her little one and bleats in grief for some time. Eventually, she has to move on," Grandpa said with a sadness in his eyes, though he knew that that was the way nature worked.

He noticed his granddaughter's tender, broken heart and quivering frown. He wrapped his strong arm around Alta Fay. Grandpa pulled her close as she wiped tears away that had escaped in a stream down her young, rosy cheek.

"I hope nothing bad ever happens to Dottie, Grandpa," said Alta Fay.

"I can't promise you anything, Alta. Dottie is a wild animal and I can't be penning her up. It wouldn't be right," Grandpa stated.

Alta did her best to understand. The girls continued stroking the fawn's sleek coat until it was time to go weeding again. It felt comfortable having grandpa sit with them. He wasn't as busy as Daddy seemed to always be. He acted interested in what interested them. This included their compassion toward the fawn. Dottie was doted over so much by all of the family that she eventually became as friendly and loved as a pet dog.

Chapter 10

The Narrow Escape

As Phyllis approached Big Grandma's one morning she noticed that Dottie was lying in the grass near the yard swing. Phyllis sauntered over toward the swing and the fawn immediately jumped up and followed her.

"What in the world are you up to?" Phyllis asked, half to herself and half to Dottie. She soon saw that if she took a couple of steps and stopped, the fawn would do the same. It was a smart deer and wanted to play.

Alta Fay had arrived earlier to Grandma's and was finishing up a piece of toast when she heard Phyllis. Drawing the curtain aside and peering out the kitchen window, Alta Fay caught sight of her sister and bounded out of the house. She stopped briefly to observe what was going on and then joined in the fun. The girls would run a few paces and stop; so would Dottie. Then the girls turned and let the fawn run a few yards and they became the pursuers. This game lasted for nearly half an hour. Finally, the girls, exhausted and giddy, needed to end their play. Phyllis said, "We'd better get to weeding some onion rows or we're gonna be in a heap of trouble." Alta Fay agreed, and, after a loving pat on the fawn's head, the girls skipped off to work.

The brown-eyed beauty settled under the big shade tree and napped as Alta Fay and Phyllis often gazed at her with love and admiration from the onion field.

"What a wonderful creature," Alta Fay commented, half to herself and half to Phyllis. Phyllis smiled in agreement yet tried to hold back her true feelings. She hated to be negative, but, face it, something bad might happen to Dottie just as it did to Judy. *Don't get too attached,* Phyllis thought. *It will only break your heart.*

Day in and day out, the summer sped by at a racer's pace. One day, as the girls approached their grandparent's home they noticed that Grandpa was in the yard kneeling down and working on something. Grandma was busy fetching him some warm water in her wash pan. Alta Fay took off like a shot to where Grandpa was hunched over working.

"What's wrong?" Alta demanded as she nosed her way around to get a better look. What she saw was blood, and then a most gruesome sight.

Grandma, without looking up, said, "Apparently Dottie was targeted by a poacher some time during the night. Her left eye has been shot out."

Phyllis could tell from Grandma's voice that she was both hurt and disgusted. Grandma continued, "She is stunned, but it doesn't appear that she'll die." This was a great relief to the young girls, who hadn't realized how attached they had become to the fawn. Grandpa washed the fleshy opening gently and Grandma applied some of her homemade medicinal salve to the gaping wound. After dressing Dottie's wound, Grandpa made a bed in the barn for her, and the girls checked on their fawn every chance they could. Before going home Phyllis and Alta Fay rested on the soft straw in the barn beside Dottie and talked.

"Why would anyone do that, Phil?" questioned Alta Fay.

Without waiting for a response she continued. "I'd be really sad if anything were to happen to Dottie."

"Me, too," replied Phyllis. "You said that before, Alta Fay, but we cannot control what happens all the time."

"I know, Phil. I just love her so much," said Alta Fay.

"I do, too," Phyllis replied, staring off into space.

Changing the subject, Phyllis stated, "We got to be heading for home. Let's go say bye to Grandma and Grandpa."

They both leaned over and kissed Dottie on the head. Then, carefully they stood up and tiptoed out of the cool barn. Dottie was sleeping peacefully again and they didn't want to wake her.

After kissing their grandparents, the girls tramped down the steps and began their journey home. Grandma waved to them until they were down the lane and out of sight. She knew her girls would be in a rush to tell their mother all about the incident. It was quite a miracle that the deer had survived.

As soon as home was in sight, the girls took off like roadrunners. Mamma was sitting on the porch, out of the sun, rocking their little brother. "I don't think you're workin' hard enough if you can come home with this kind of energy," Mamma critiqued.

Doubled over and breathing heavily, Alta Fay explained everything, in detail, that had happened at the farm. Phyllis slouched in a chair beside Mamma, trying to catch her breath and resting her tired body.

"Well, it doesn't surprise me, Alta. There are a lot of families, like ours, in need of meat. People get desperate. We're real fortunate that Daddy has work right now and we have Grandma and Grandpa up the lane to help some," explained Mamma matter-of-factly.

"But not a baby deer, Mamma!" pleaded Alta Fay.

"I know, Alta. But everybody doesn't see it that way. You have to understand that what you are considering a pet is really a wild animal. Dottie is considered a meal for those who are trying to feed a family. These are awful tough times. Try and understand," Mamma explained.

Alta Fay did not understand, but Phyllis did. She understood it all too well. Once again, Phyllis tried to distance herself from the deer, but it had already taken up residency in her big heart, just as it did Alta Fay's. She prayed every night that Dottie would be kept safe.

Fortunately, it was only a few days before Dottie was prancing around again. The fawn seemed to wait each morning for the girls to come and play. Everything seemed to be back to normal. Even Dottie didn't appear any different until one looked at her scarred-over eye socket. This baby deer had made the summer in the onion field memorable for the young Clayton girls. That is why they were heartbroken when the onions were harvested and there was no need to travel every day to Big Grandma's house. School would soon begin again, and the girls would spend less and less time there. So every moment they could get away from chores and children, Phyllis and Alta Fay ran to their grandparents to visit and play with Dottie.

What a magnificent summer it had been for the young girls. There would be many stories to share with their schoolhouse friends. Not many children could boast of having a pet deer! For once, the Clayton family would be the envy of the valley.

Chapter 11

Death

ONE OF THE LAST DAYS before school was to begin, the girls approached Grandma and Grandpa Blanchard's house and saw Big Grandma waiting, fidgeting nervously on the front porch steps. They both wondered what was wrong. Alta seemed to know instinctively that it was Dottie. Phyllis and Alta Fay looked at each other in confusion, stopped at the bottom of the steps, and stared up at Big Grandma. She gazed down at her grandchildren, but had to quickly look away. She had no smile for them today.

Big Grandma wrung her hands on a dishtowel like she had just finished washing dishes, though Phyllis thought it was her way of relieving the stress she was feeling. It was difficult for Grandma to maintain eye contact with the girls because it brought tears so easily to her eyes. She was fighting both tears of pain and tears of anger. Phyllis later learned that this combination makes for the worst kind of hurt. It strains a person mentally and physically.

Finally, though, Grandma quietly explained what had happened. "Dottie has not come around this morning and Grandpa heard a shot in the night. Poachers must have killed her is all we can think."

Both girls stood in shocked silence. Finally, Big Grandma continued talking, "What makes Dottie's disappearance worse is that everyone in the valley knows about her and how much the little deer means to our families." Grandma's face was turning bright red, and the intensity of her emotions was escalating to a feverish pitch. "I'll tell you there's that monkey-baboon of a family down in the old swale that would shoot at anything that moved. They're just the type that would have thought it great sport to have shot Dottie, the pet deer, and have eaten her for their dinner, just to spite us!"

Grandpa knew just whom it was that Big Grandma was speaking of, though they would not disclose the information to their tender-eared grandchildren. However, as a matter of support for his wife's opinion, he added, "Worse yet, Agnes, those people own cattle and are never short of meat! I tell ya,' Agnes, this was not a matter of need, but plain and simple, a matter of pure meanness." This terrible act of cruelty was something that neither a child nor any compassionate adult would ever be able to understand.

"I'm real sorry, girls, that your deer is gone. It's hard to understand why these things happen. She probably would have run away pretty soon anyway. Like I said before, a person can't keep a wild animal penned up. It just ain't right," Grandpa said, trying to console them.

Still, the fact remained that their lovely pet was gone forever. Dottie's death profoundly affected Alta Fay. Often, she sat quietly contemplating death in her young, innocent mind. Sometimes she would share her thoughts with Phyllis concerning such abstract matters.

"Where do deer go when they die?" Alta wondered.

"I'm not sure. Probably to heaven," Phyllis replied. She really had no way of answering these questions with one hundred percent certainty.

"Big deer die all of the time, but not little deer," pondered Alta. "Why is that? It doesn't seem right. That fawn didn't even have a chance to live its life, Phil," Alta sobbed.

"I'm not sure about a lot of things, Alta, but I know that it must have been in God's plan, and we have to accept that," Phyllis was startled by her own words. She thought, *So this is what Mother must feel like when she tries explaining things to us kids.* Phyllis felt a little more grown up.

With renewed confidence, Phyllis ordered Alta Fay, "Come with me. I have an idea."

Alta Fay shook her head in solemn agreement, though she still wasn't quite sure about the whole "God's plan" explanation. Maybe some day she would understand completely.

In the meantime, she and Phyllis were on a mission. In order to accomplish the mission, they must first find their Grandpa, who was last seen heading toward the house.

"Grandpa, can we make a wooden cross for Dottie?" Phyllis let Alta Fay ask. Grandpa, pouring himself a cup of coffee, smiled meekly, ruffled Alta's hair and said to her, "I'll go see what I got up in the barn after I finish this here cup."

The girls sat anxiously with him until he tipped the cup to retrieve the last few drops, minus the grounds that were hiding in the bottom. Phyllis and Alta Fay followed outside. They were so closely on his heels that if he had had to stop, they would have run into his backside. Up at the barn, he found two wooden stakes, expertly sharpened the end of one, tacked the two together to form a small, rugged cross, and presented it to the girls for inspection and approval. Grandma Blanchard found some old paint and ragged brushes and allowed the girls plenty of time to work on their memorial. While the paint was drying, Phyllis, Alta, and Grandma had a glass of weak tea on the cool porch. After checking on the progress of the drying paint several times, the trio, finally satisfied, carried the cross to the shade tree where Dottie had always rested. Alta Fay carefully pounded it into the ground using a large rock as a make-shift hammer. Tears were streaming down all of their cheeks. Grandma solemnly promised, "I'll be sure and leave Dottie's cross here forever. I loved that little deer, too." Grandma's voice was racked with emotion. The girls kept quiet. It was upsetting to see their Big Grandma so sad. It was a side of Grandma they were not used to seeing, and they were unsure of what to do or say to her. Big Grandma's sadness reflected and intensified their sadness.

Phyllis and Alta Fay did not run home this day. Grandma had sent them with a fresh batch of buttermilk cookies, a long, thoughtful hug, and a butterfly kiss. They slowly made their way down the dusty road in silence. Both of the girls needed time to think, and this was the best time to do it. They had lost a friend and playmate, reminding Phyllis once again of life's uncertainties.

Chapter 12

Grandpa and the Farmers' Almanac

WITH SCHOOL WELL UNDER WAY, the girls had little time to think of anything else. It was chores, schoolwork, dinner, and bed. Times were hard and Daddy wouldn't ask for help, so often the dinner part was miniscule, at best. The girls often went to bed hungry. Their favorite day was Sunday because Grandpa and Grandma Blanchard drove the shires down and picked Mamma and the children up for church. The music was inspiring and on warm Sunday mornings when the windows were open, the small congregation's rendition of "In the Sweet By and By" lilted playfully on the breeze. Phyllis knew that afterwards her grandparents would be invited to Sunday dinner at the Clayton house. Grandma always baked bread, dinner rolls, cinnamon rolls, and brought along a huge container of potato salad for this occasion. That way Phyllis's father would think that it was more of a potluck than Grandma helping them out. Maybe he knew better, but would not say anything for fear his ego may starve. Phyllis loved her daddy, but, oh, was he a stubborn one. Grandma always claimed it was the German in him. Phyllis had her doubts.

It was after Sunday dinner in the early part of October of every year that Grandpa Blanchard would attempt to be the weather forecaster for the upcoming winter. He sat on the Clayton's second-hand sofa, smoking his pipe as he lectured, passing on his indispensable wisdom of nature to the children who had gathered around his feet.

"Yep," he said confidently. "I never saw hair thickern' what I saw on those there animals of ours. In fact, on the way home from town I noticed that the muskrat houses down on Sand Creek are extra large this year. It's gonna be a cold, snowy one. That's the way I see it, and if I'm wrong I'll eat the greaser."

That saying of Grandpa Blanchard's turned Phyllis's stomach. The greaser was a big piece of bacon skin and fat that people used to grease the pancake griddle with every morning.

"Eeew, Grandpa," Phyllis protested. "Who'd eat that old thing?"

"You'd be surprised what people will eat when they're near starvin'," Grandpa sternly stated. "I remember my daddy being so hungry that he ate the bark off of a tree!"

Phyllis and the other children stared without speaking. Grandpa had become very serious and they dared not make a sound. The memories he just shared sounded like something that agitated him. It was difficult for Grandpa to discuss.

After pausing to reflect about a very tough time, Grandpa Blanchard smiled, knowing well that the children couldn't understand how memories can hurt, and continued the tales, many of which held much credence. "If the smoke from a chimney is blowing toward the ground, or if the leaves on the trees are turned over, then you can tell it's gonna rain."

Grandma had been quietly rocking one of the babies while she listened to her husband. She became caught up in the excitement and added a few of her own old wives' tales she had learned through the years. The children all turned to face her as she spoke. "If you're bothered with cramps, turn your shoes upside down before goin' to bed.

"What's cramps, Grandma?" asked Alta Fay.

Without skipping a beat, Big Grandma replied, "Well, some people get cramps in their feet." She then held up her foot and pointed to the underside of the arch, and continued, "The muscles in here are pullin' and a twistin' every which way. It is real painful."

Expanding on her mini lecture, Grandma added, "Sometimes you can get a cramp in your belly when you have to use the toilet or you got the flu bug."

"Oh, I've got those before and they feel awful," Alta Fay said with a grimace.

Grandma smiled. "Yes, but it's usually not too long and the hurtin' is over."

She thought it best not to discuss female cramps until her grandgirls were older. Both eager to avoid the topic and relieved that Alta Fay was satisfied with the first two "cramp" explanations, Grandma Blanchard continued with another saying. "If a bird flies in your house, there's gonna be a death in the family."

Phyllis could tell Grandma wished she hadn't added that last old wives' tale when she looked at all the saucer round eyes staring up at her. All of the children's mouths were hanging open, and a couple of them puckered up as if they would cry at any moment. Big Grandma waved her hand in the air as if she could somehow erase what she had just said. "Don't you fret none. Those are just old tales. They're not really true."

Collectively, the older children sighed in relief and the younger children calmed down. Grandma was glad to have settled that matter and vowed to herself she would think twice before doing that again. She soon went on to tell some happy stories from her childhood, and her grandchildren sat quietly, admiring their wonderful Grandma. Grandpa was more than glad to rest and listen. He leaned back in his chair. Two of the children crawled up on his lap and quickly fell asleep.

By the end of October, Grandpa's predictions were already coming to pass. It had snowed early and it wasn't even Halloween yet. In fact, it was October 29, 1933, and Phyllis was turning eight years old. Her mamma had roasted two chickens and had made some dumplings in the bubbling broth. This was Phyllis's favorite, once a year meal. Grandpa and Grandma Blanchard came down and shared in the feast. Daddy had traded some cement work labor for the chickens. Big Grandma baked the cake because she was able to barter vegetables for the ingredients. It had a dark chocolate bottom with a rich, chocolate frosting. She even had some store-bought candles to place on top! Daddy got a couple of blocks of ice and made homemade ice cream using a borrowed, hand turn freezer. After everyone had his or her share, Daddy played the harmonica for them. The children skipped around the living room. It was a wonderful birthday. Mamma had knitted Phyllis a beautiful pink sweater to replace her ruined red one.

"Don't you go leaving this by any pigs," she smiled.

Phyllis laughed. Grandma rested in a chair near her granddaughter when she opened the next gift. Before Phyllis could find out what she had received, Grandma was jabbering and apologizing. "I sure hope you like the color. I didn't have many colors to choose from."

Phyllis quickly tore open the package and held up a scarf and mittens that Grandma had handmade just for her.

"They should keep you warm on your way to and from the schoolhouse," Grandma explained.

"Thank you, Grandma," Phyllis said as she hugged her grandma.

"I'll thank Grandpa when he quits snoozing," she giggled.

Grandpa had fallen asleep in the chair in the other room after dinner was finished. He did not mind being left out. He liked to rest when he had the chance.

"Thanks Mamma. Thanks Daddy," she embraced each one, in turn, and softly kissed them. Phyllis had never known such attention before. She felt like a queen. It had been a supreme birthday, and the fun had not ended yet.

A few days later, Daddy brought the children into town for Halloween trick-or-treating, and they gathered a small bag of goodies each and then returned home. Mamma stayed with the babies and was happy to be given a break. That night, just before turning in from the evening's events, Daddy went out to use the outhouse. Unbeknownst to him, Alta Fay was hiding in the bushes beside the toilet, and as soon as he was close enough she pushed an old stuffed coyote head out so that its lifeless, tooth-bearing mouth touched his leg. "AAHHHH!" he screamed, and he kicked the head clear up to the front steps of the house. In the darkness, Daddy stood, catching his breath and waiting for his heart to stop racing. As everything was calming down and the yard became quiet again, he heard a giggle coming from behind the bushes. Suddenly, Alta Fay appeared, doubled over laughing. "Good one, huh, Dad?" bragged Alta Fay.

Daddy pretended to be mad at her, but he knew she had just scared him real good. "You get over here young lady," said Daddy in a pretend angry voice. He ran to Alta, picked her up like a sack of potatoes, threw her over his shoulder, and carried her to the house giggling. No one ever saw that coyote head again.

That evening George plunked himself down on the edge of Phyllis and Alta Fay's bed and told them a short story that this night's events had stirred in his memory. Several times he had to stop his story and order the girls to stop giggling over the coyote head incident.

After regaining their composure for the second or third time, George began, "I remember when we lived in an upstairs apartment. Well, it was a week or so after Halloween, and the jack-o-lantern that we had carved was still sitting on the balcony railing becoming softer and more rotten each day. My mother had yelled at us to take it out back and throw it in the woods, but we got busy and it still hadn't gotten done. Anyway, one night I left the house on my way to see your ma. And as I walked out onto the porch, your Uncle Ike, who was still up on the balcony, took that pumpkin, held it directly over my head, and let it go. It hit me square on top of the head, and, because it was rotten, it smashed right down onto my shoulders. I was left with a nasty pumpkin collar around my neck. Boy, was I glad that it was rotten 'cause if it wasn't, I'd have been knocked out cold for sure!" George grinned then continued, "You must have got your prankster-mind from your Uncle Ike, Alta Fay."

Without saying anything, George leaned over and began tickling the girls until tears of laughter streamed down their faces. When he finally stopped tickle-torturing the girls, he stood up and said, "Now, you two jokers get some sleep." He gave each daughter a peck on the cheek and quietly left the room.

Alta Fay could not contain her giggles as she recalled the entire evening's events, including her dad's pumpkin story. Under the covers Phyllis would beg her to tell the stories once more. Both girls would be repeatedly seized by uncontrollable fits of laughter. These would be a couple more stories that Alta Fay could add to her collection that she shared with her younger siblings.

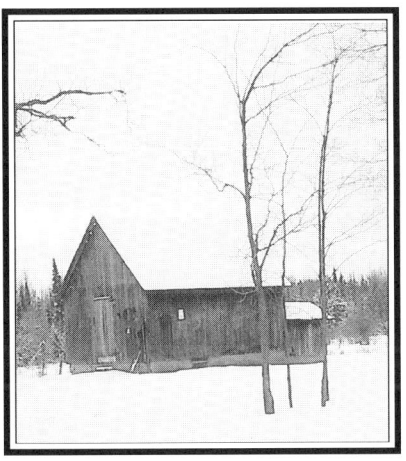

Chapter 13

The Pocketknife

November was cold and snowy, but December came in like a lamb. It was unseasonably warm, and most of the snow that had accumulated during the last month disappeared.

Pine trees around Sand Creek were scarce, so, for Christmas, the Clayton family filled a pail with sand and stuck a big branch into the middle of it for a makeshift tree. Mamma popped and strung some corn, and the children made paper ornaments to hang on the tree-branch. It was simple but beautiful. The grand shires trekked Grandpa and Grandma down to Christmas dinner by sleigh.

They had brought each of the children a small gift. Christmas was scant, at best, and the children were told that Santa was experiencing tough times during this Depression and not to expect much. They didn't. So, it was a surprisingly glorious moment when, off in the corner of the room, Phyllis carefully opened her brown, paper-wrapped gift and discovered that it was a beautiful ivory handled pocketknife.

"Oh my goodness," she burst out ecstatically. "This is the nicest present I've ever gotten!" Immediately her mind became a whirr. She could see herself whittling a stick into a tiny spear and trying to catch a fish down at Betcher Creek. She thought about carving her initials into a smooth barked beech tree. Maybe she would even carve Barbara's initials and Barbara's boyfriend's initials into a tree. Phyllis smiled at that last thought. Barbara would act embarrassed, but would secretly be proud to say her beloved is Mr. Fredrick Beecher. She delighted in the thought of being addressed one day as Mrs. Fredrick Beecher.

All of the other girls smiled and hugged Grandma after receiving a lovely, hand-made shawl. When Alta Fay saw what Phyllis had gotten she couldn't believe her eyes. She really liked her shawl and didn't want a pocketknife, but she knew that Phyllis surely would. She smiled and hugged her. "Do you think I could use it sometime, Phil?" whispered Alta Fay quietly into her ear.

"Sure you can, Alta," replied Phyllis. "I share everything with you."

A few moments later, though, Jonathon opened a shawl and the family realized that someone had received the wrong gift. They gazed around the room until their eyes fell upon Phyllis and Alta Fay. Phyllis wanted to hide the knife, but she knew it wasn't the right thing to do, so she just stood there unable to move and just stared meekly back. The adults, without knowing the harm it would cause, approached Phyllis, took the beautiful object from her limp hands, and exchanged the gifts. To them it was a simple mistake and the matter was settled. No one bothered to notice the pale, sickly look that had come over Phyllis's face, except Alta Fay.

"Couldn't you get Johnny another knife and let Phyllis keep this one?" Alta Fay loudly and pleadingly asked, although she knew neither family could afford the extravagance.

The entire gathering of people paused and turned to gawk at Alta Fay, then at Phyllis, not quite believing what they had just heard. *The audacity of this child,* their faces seemed to accuse. *How dare she question any gift!* Phyllis, with her eyes fixed on the floor, was attempting to hold back the tears, but Alta Fay, her hands on her hips, was on the warpath.

"Alta Fay, you know perfectly well that a young lady has no use for a pocketknife," commented Mamma, as she turned her body to face her daughter directly. "Phyllis had better appreciate this beautiful shawl. Grandma made it with all her love." Turning back to the other adults, the matter was settled in Mother's mind, and the merry making continued. Big Grandma did not intervene because it was not her place. Though she was not necessarily in full agreement, she would not meddle.

Phyllis did like the shawl and knew that her grandma had spent a great deal of time making it, but, truthfully, she would rather have had the pocketknife. That was all there was to it for this eight-year-old child. Her intention was not to act unappreciatively, especially toward Grandma. Phyllis was deeply hurt and disappointed. Alta Fay silently remained by her sister's side for the rest of the evening.

Later that night, under the covers of their bed, Alta Fay whispered, "I would buy you a pocketknife if I could, Phil."

Phyllis was softly crying, partly because she was still hurting, partly because Mamma now thought of her as unappreciative of Grandma's gift. But mostly the tears fell because Alta Fay, so little and feisty, had acted so unselfishly and strong. She was not sure she would have been as strong had the situation been reversed. It touched Phyllis's heart in a special way.

Years later, Phyllis would recall, it wasn't the pocketknife that had been the best thing about the Christmas of '33; it was the privilege of having known her loyal and loving sister and playmate, Alta Fay.

Chapter 14

The Cold Winiter

JANUARY WAS SNOWY, AND THE Clayton family saw less and less of Grandma and Grandpa Blanchard. It was too difficult for the old couple to get out. Even if the road was plowed, the Blanchard's feared their only two workhorses could become injured by a fall on the slippery road. They had what food they needed right there on the farm, so unless one or the other became ill, it would be some time before they came to visit again.

The children missed them, and after the V-Plow tractor was able to open up the road, the four oldest girls bundled up as best they could and walked to their grandparent's home for a visit. The briskly paced walk warmed them up quite well.

"What in the world are you girls doing out on a stormy day like today?" Big Grandma asked as she gathered her grandchildren into her kitchen on this gray winter's day.

"We missed you, Grandma. And Mamma said we could come and visit for a while," stated Clare.

"I was missing you all as well," Grandma replied as she helped them take off their winter clothes and hung them to dry by the woodstove. "Grandpa's got an awful cold in his chest and is lying down. He just went to sleep before you got here. He'll be sorry he didn't get a chance to visit with you."

"Is he gonna be O.K., Grandma?" Alta Fay worriedly inquired.

"Oh, yes, Alta. He'll be fine. He gets this every winter 'bout this time," reassured Grandma.

The girls sat around the kitchen table, drank tea, and ate scones with Grandma. She told them stories and inquired about the family. The cat curled up in Phyllis's lap, and Alta Fay sat close, rubbing its soft head. It must have felt safe and warm because it purred loudly as it napped. Running in and out-of-doors was not so popular this cold, wretched time of year, so the door had been slammed fewer times on the cat.

The few wonderful hours ticked away quickly. It seemed that the girls had just arrived when the time came to leave. Barbara stood and said, "We've got to be getting home, Grandma. Tell Grandpa we said hello."

Grandma nodded. "Time flies don't it girls?" she commented. Then she advised her granddaughters, "You remember that the older you get, the faster time flies."

The girls shook their heads in recognition of her comment, but could not truly understand because they had not lived long enough yet. To a child, time crawls along at a snail's pace, and any other view of life is inconceivable. Inevitably, time will be their sole teacher.

As Grandma helped the girls into their warm clothes she said, "I'd like you all to stay, but your mamma will be lookin' for you to be home 'fore dark sets in." Grandma was the worried one. She did not like to have her grandkids out after dark. She was always worrying. She treated it like an innate responsibility of any loving grandparent.

Not understanding Grandma's worry, the girls giggled and rolled their eyes as if it were all silliness. What could possibly happen to them between Grandma's house and their house?

Without noticing the humor she was providing for her granddaughters, Grandma remembered and added, "You be careful and watch for cars."

"We will, Grandma," answered the girls, holding back more giggles.

The girls dressed quickly, kissed their wonderful Grandma, and tramped out into the cold. Phyllis had left the sleeping cat on Grandpa's chair so it would be safe from the door.

"Good-bye, Grams," Alta Fay yelled back as she sped ahead of the other three on her way back home. Barbara and Clare paid Alta Fay no mind, but Phyllis picked up her skirt and streaked after her comrade. She wasn't about to back down from Alta's silent challenge. Phyllis seemed to always come in second in foot races against Alta Fay, but she didn't mind.

It wasn't two shakes of a coon's tail before they both burst through the door of their home calling out, in unison, "I won! I won!" Each wanted to be the first to hang up their wet coat and boots. They had actually begun to sweat from the run, and it would feel good to take off their sticky clothes. Barbara and Clare came in several minutes later.

"You girls stomp your boots off before you come in my house. I just cleaned up the last mess from your father just a bit ago," Mamma yelled in a sick-and-tired-of-cleaning-up-after-people attitude.

"You just made it in time for dinner," Mamma remarked as she set a plate of mashed potatoes in the center of the table. Daddy looked hard at the girls. "You cannot leave every other day to visit Grandpa and Grandma Blanchard while your Mamma is working so hard without any help here at home."

"I let them go, George," Mary defensively stated. "They needed some fresh air."

"You're too easy on 'em, Mary. You need help and they're old enough to provide a bit more of it," George commented.

"They do, George. You know they do," continued Mary.

George scooped up a heap of potatoes and passed the bowl around, giving no more of a scolding. He had said his piece, did his duty, and expected the girls to amend the situation immediately, no questions asked. The girls knew this.

Barbara broke the silence and said, "Sorry, Daddy. We won't go up there for a while."

Mamma hugged the girls, one by one, and said sincerely, "Thank you," as she kissed them on the top of their head. "I hate to ask you kids to grow up so fast. You shouldn't have to spend all of your time here watching the little ones and helping out. I know you dearly love Big Grandma and Grandpa and love to see them. I've just had a 'specially bad day, and Daddy is just trying to help me out. All we're asking for are a few extra daily chores to be done before you go." With that Mamma sat down and dished up a plate of food for each of the little ones and finally a plate for herself.

Clare stood and walked over to Mamma and kissed her on the cheek, saying, "We didn't realize, Mamma, how much you needed us."

Mamma began to softly cry. The girls were certain that this wasn't the first time she had broken down today. She pushed her food around on her plate as tears fell quietly onto the table. She was unable to eat in this frame of mind. It wasn't an angry cry, but a sad and exhausted one. Sometimes she wished that she was still a child and could let her mother take care of her.

Big Grandma did, in many ways, do this, but Mamma needed to get away from it all. She loved her family, but often wished she had finished school and then went to college. She had always wanted to become a nurse. Mamma did not like being so dependent on George. With no money, lack of time, and no encouragement, Mamma had little in the way of options. Her dreams would never come to pass. She couldn't drive a car, and, even if she could, she had no place to go. Sad and tired, Mamma sat with her head bent down, staring at the handkerchief she was fidgeting with in her hands. The family ate quietly. None of them knew what to do for her, so they remained uncomfortably silent.

"Once I get to bed and have a good night's rest, I'll be all right," declared Mamma, half-heartedly and wholly defeated.

Chapter 15

Snow Days

DADDY PUT THE CHILDREN TO bed that night. He tucked each of them in and gave them a soft kiss. It was an unusual treat that the children enjoyed. George then made sure the kitchen was in order and helped his wife up from her chair, hugged her, and walked her to their bedroom. She quietly dressed in her night-clothes, and George pulled back the blankets and helped her to lie down. Finally, he kissed her for a long time and rubbed her head. "I love you. Get some sleep. The kids are all tucked in and I'm just going to sit up for a while. Good night."

That night all of the Clayton children fell into a deep and contented sleep. Daddy would take care of their mamma, and he still loved all of them.

George sat in his big old leather chair and read the paper for a time before turning in for the night. Some time later, Phyllis awoke and heard her father mention quietly to her mother, "It looks like there might be quite a storm coming in from the northwest, lots of snow."

Phyllis could picture him standing near their bed, looking out into the night. He then regrettably added, "The children will probably need to stay home from school tomorrow. It won't be much of a break for you I know."

Phyllis could not hear Mamma's response because, long before Daddy went to bed, Mamma was in a deep, much needed sleep. But Phyllis was sure that having all the kids stay home on account of a snowstorm was a small obstacle for her strong mamma. With her daughters' help she could handle the mission easily. Truth be known, Phyllis thought it was Daddy, who was out of work and trapped at home until spring, who would have a tough time with it. Sure enough, Daddy was right. It snowed all night and most of the next day. Nothing was moving but the cold, winter winds.

Many days the road to the tiny shack of a home in the valley did not get plowed until late afternoon or evening, if at all. When the children remained home from school, they played pretend school, along with checkers, marbles, and Cats-in-the-Cradle. There were also many chores to be done, diapers to be changed, and babies to be soothed. As Daddy had predicted, the Clayton house was thoroughly chaotic. Mamma handled it well. Daddy was frazzled by the time it was over. He searched for any excuse to desert to the barn for a while.

It was a welcomed time when the roads were cleared and the children were able to get back to school. Everything was less hectic for Mamma and Daddy on those days.

January was bitterly cold, but February seemed to be slightly warmer. It had not snowed and was pleasant for most of the month. When the chores had been done, Alta Fay and Phyllis spent much of their free time traveling to Big Grandma's to visit. Barbara and Clare enjoyed remaining indoors where it was warm. They only ventured out occasionally. Daddy was satisfied with the extra duties the girls were doing for their mother at home, so he stopped complaining. It was a welcome relief to leave the noisy house behind for a few hours. Grandma spoiled her granddaughters with baked goods each trip they made, and she never sent them home empty handed. Mary and her family appreciated her mother's generosity.

Chapter 16

The Storm

THE WINTER APPEARED TO BE letting up and would give the battered valley a much needed rest. However, typical of Michigan weather, that hope was short-lived. By the end of the month a snowstorm like no other that had been seen in many a year fell from the heavens in a fitful rage. The once rested valley was now beginning to be buried under a deep white blanket of snow.

The blizzard began late that afternoon, roaring through the valley like an angry freight train. The skeleton-like branches on the trees groaned under the weight of the newly fallen snow. No one was coming in nor going out in this violent weather. Life had seemed to come to a halt. Worse yet, the large family seemed to be coming down with an ailment of sorts. Alta Fay complained, "Mamma, I have a terrible stomachache."

"It's probably the flu," replied Mother. "You kids have been stuck indoors for so long the air has become stale and has been breeding germs by the bushel basket." Mamma made sure to keep an eye on Alta Fay, though. She always believed that one could never be too careful when it came to the children. On the other hand, she didn't want to make a fuss over a minor, seasonal ailment if that is all it was. It would just cause undo stress on the rest of the large family.

Throughout the evening, as the winter storm raged outside, Alta Fay lay shivering with pain and fever beneath one of her mother's patchwork quilts. She gratefully, but weakly mumbled, "Thanks, Phil." Phyllis had been patiently bringing Alta Fay cool water and caringly helped her repeatedly stagger back and forth between the pot and warm bed. Phyllis felt that serving as a makeshift nurse was the least she could do for her brave and loyal sister. As Phyllis removed and rinsed the cloth that lay pressed against Alta's burning forehead, she decided that she would tell Alta Fay a story to bide the slow-moving time.

"Do you remember last year's Easter morning, Alta?" asked Phyllis as she stroked her sister's soft cheek. "You thought it would be helpful to us kids if you got up real early, before the rest of the family, and gathered all of the eggs that the Easter Bunny left.

Holding up her hands like she was showing someone what she had hidden in the folds of her apron, Phyllis reenacted the scene. She enthusiastically attempted to imitate Alta Fay's voice saying, "Look everybody!"

Phyllis quietly continued. "You proudly opened your apron and showed us what you'd found. Every single Easter egg was in there. I knew that you thought what you'd done was helping us, so you couldn't understand why we were so mad. It was really pretty funny when I think back."

Phyllis's smile faded as Alta's weak cry of pain brought her back to reality. Her illness had worsened to the point that she was unable to respond to the Easter-egg story. Phyllis was unsure whether Alta Fay even heard it.

When Mamma hustled in to check on Alta's condition for what seemed the hundredth time, she noticed that there was a bluish tint to her pale skin. Instinctively, Mamma knew it was something more than a seasonal flu that was ravaging the frail body of her young child.

Mary's mother and her Grandma Kingsley taught her about several home remedies when she was growing up. One such remedy for helping a youngster with an earache was to put warm oil or a few drops of warm urine into the aching ear. She learned to make a spring tonic of sassafras tea and to calm her restless children by having them drink a warm cup of catnip tea. For a chest cold she could mix turpentine with lard and rub it on the chest, then place a piece of flannel over it. If she didn't have that combination, she could use a mustard and flour mixture, make a plaster, and apply it to the chest.

However effective Mamma's home remedies could be, at this moment, they were of no use to Alta Fay. In a way, Mamma was like the mother deer that stood to the side, helplessly looking on, as extreme sickness preyed upon her baby. She could do nothing for her sick little girl but love her and pray for her. Mamma dropped to her knees and pleaded, "Dear God, let my baby be healed. I will take her place. Please God, please…" The tears in her eyes blurred her vision, but she had to try to remain strong and positive so the other children would not become upset. She lowered her head to hide her pain until she regained some composure.

At Mamma's beckoning, Daddy had left over an hour ago, on foot, to call the doctor from the nearest neighbor's house.

This neighbor was the town supervisor, and he was the closest one who had a phone. However, the snow was hip-deep, and the mile and a half journey was both painfully slow and treacherous. George was exhausted and to the point of hyperventilation by the time he reached his destination.

Although George and this supervisor had had their differences in the past, Alta Fay's well-being brought them together, and each had done his share in getting help to the Clayton home. Once George was assured that help was on its way, he set off again, at an Olympic runner's pace, to get back to his little girl. His legs would not trudge through the snow fast enough. His mind was swirling and racing the mile ahead, while dragging his legs behind.

After another quarter of an hour, which seemed to Phyllis and the others like an eternity, the family finally heard their daddy stomping his boots at the front door before coming in. Mamma met him, tears of worry and relief clouding her troubled eyes. With both hands, Mamma grabbed and held onto Daddy's chest. His plaid shirt was bunched in each of her fists. This held him still as she inquired, "Is he coming? When will he get here? He's got to come quick! Alta Fay's circulation isn't too good! She's got to be seen by the doctor…" Mamma went on not waiting to hear Daddy's answers.

Daddy touched Mamma's lips with his fingertips to calm her down and stop her from rambling on with worry.

"I spoke with the doctor. He's doing his best to get out here, but the storm is really hinderin' him," Daddy said dismally as he placed his strong hands on both of hers and lowered them from his chest so they rested, once again, by her sides. He held them for a moment and then hugged her. They had no choice but to wait for the doctor.

This dedicated elderly man had been present for most of the births in this county. He had cared for entire families through the scarlet fever, whooping cough, pneumonia, and the mumps epidemics. He had seen more than his share of tragic, untimely deaths. Though it appeared impossible for him to reach the Clayton home due to the deep snow, he could not give up on this child, or any other person that he knew was experiencing a health crisis. His conscience would not allow this, nor would his heart.

George tried to keep his impatience at bay by pacing the room. He continued to provide Mary with more bits of information about his conversation with the doctor.

"The town supervisor told me he'd try to get a hold of the county road commission. I wasn't gonna leave until I knew for sure some help was on the way. After a while he got through by telephone and a plow tractor was called out to clear the road up here to the house. That's the only way the Doc's old Model T can get to Alta Fay."

After a few tense moments, Daddy became more fidgety and said in an angry, tired tone, "I sure wish they'd hurry up!"

The news of the doctor's coming sparked hope in Mamma's heart, and she waited eagerly next to the window, peering out into the blackness until she saw the round, yellow headlights piercing the darkness. At first came the mammoth V-Plow, but right behind it came another set of lights. They were beacons of hope for this desperate family.

Daddy was in checking on Alta Fay when he heard Mamma yell to the rest of the family, "He's here! The Doctor has made it! Oh, thank you, God!" Mary said, gazing up toward the heavens. She was ready and waiting at the door within seconds.

The anxious mother pulled the snow-covered man into her humble home. Mamma's brief words were, "So glad to see you, Doc! Alta's this way." She grabbed his coat, threw it haphazardly over a chair, and led him quickly into her daughter's room. This was one of those moments that require no formalities. Phyllis stood up, managing to produce a shaky but polite smile, and made room for the doctor to observe Alta Fay. She remained respectfully silent.

"How long has Alta been ill?" he questioned.

Phyllis replied for her Mamma, "Since yesterday. She's been drinkin' so much water and havin' the diarrhea and a fever. We can hardly touch her belly without her yellin' out somethin' awful."

The doctor pressed the back of his chubby hand against Alta Fay's tiny, damp head. Next, he checked her hands and arms, peered into her feverish eyes, and then gently touched her side. Though barely conscious, Alta screamed weakly in pain. He looked up at Mamma and said matter-of-factly, "She has appendicitis, and I must drive her at once to Ann Arbor for surgery."

The family was shocked, but Mamma, in her naturally strong, in-charge manner, scurried about, gathering the necessary items for her child's trip. Daddy gingerly wrapped up Alta Fay in Mamma's heavy quilt, being careful not to aggravate her pain any more than was necessary, and carried her to the doctor's warm, idling car. In silence, the large family loomed soberly at the window watching the Model T drive off into the cold, dark night. Phyllis had desperately wanted to accompany Alta Fay to the hospital, but she was needed at home to tend to the younger children. Phyllis hoped, even though Alta Fay was fighting her own battle and was floating in and out of consciousness, that she knew her big sister wanted to be with her, to hold her, care for her and love her. Did Alta know? There was nothing more to do but wait and pray…wait and pray…

The doctor's forehead was creased with heavy wrinkles from the stress and strain of attempting to see through the frosty windshield and blinding snow. He talked to himself, complaining and worrying incessantly that he could not drive as fast as he needed to, and that Alta Fay's sickness was far too advanced. He was certain that her appendix had already ruptured, and it seemed that she was becoming weaker by the moment. About half way through the journey, Alta Fay shivered and made a deep, final sighing sound that the doctor knew all too well. He immediately pulled off to the side of the road. Alta Fay's small body lay lifeless against the seat. The doctor laid his soft hands on her small head and caressed it as his body shook with uncontrollable sobs. "No, Alta Fay. You can't just die like this. You're just a kid!" reasoned the doctor. He was exhausted and his tender heart was broken. In anger he thought, "Why do these damn country folk wait so long to come for help? Why are people so stubborn and foolish?" He knew it could have happened to any family, but it did not lessen his anger. For the moment, it was how he would cope with this loss.

After some time had passed, the good doctor wiped away his tears and gently straightened and covered Alta tenderly with her mamma's quilt.

Chapter 17

A Sorrowful Journey Home

THE DRIVE BACK TO THE Clayton home was difficult. The storm had picked up intensity, and the burden of what the old doctor had to face in a few more miles was almost too much to bear. A lifetime of training and experience was not enough to make this aspect of his profession any easier. He genuinely loved people, especially children. He had been married fifty wonderful years and had eight children of his own, along with several grandchildren and great-grandchildren. He had only recently come out of retirement after his dear, sweet wife, Josephine, had died suddenly the previous May. By continuing to work, he kept his mind from the pain of losing her. Helping those in need gave him another reason to live. He had chosen to continue making a difference in his community. The part of the job that he most dreaded, however, was being the bearer of bad news.

The doctor had been gone only a few hours when once again he turned slowly into the driveway of the Clayton home. The bright headlights brought the entire family quickly to the door. "Why has the Doc brought Alta back so soon?" questioned Phyllis.

The doctor slowly emerged from the car, trudged through the heavy snow to the passenger side, and carefully opened the door. He bent over, fumbled awkwardly, and then stood up, cradling the bundled child in his arms. In shock, the family stared at the doctor as he lumbered through the snow toward the house. Shaking himself from a daze, Daddy realized that the old man was struggling, so he began slipping his old boots on before heading out to help him. For a second, he lost his balance and hopped on one foot as he pulled on the other boot. Without bothering to put a coat on, he barreled out into the cold and took the front porch steps two at a time as he rushed to his baby. Daddy reached out to gather his little girl to himself. He lovingly held her and nestled his face into her tiny body as he rocked from side to side. The doctor's tear-filled, tired old eyes told it all. He remained speechless and still, gazing at the scene before him. Likewise, the reality of the situation was inconceivable to this shocked family. Like water being poured onto a stone, the truth was a dark stain, visible, but unable to sink in. How could a perfectly healthy child be running through the snow one day and die the next?

The children stepped timidly but reverently aside as Daddy carried Alta Fay, wrapped in the quilt, to her bed. Mamma followed him like a shadow, a dark silhouette of grief and despair. In Mamma's mind, Alta Fay needed her. Desperately, she stretched out her arms as if she had some control and could reach out to bring her baby girl back from death's grip. Many years later Phyllis realized that it wasn't Alta Fay who needed Mamma; it was Mamma who needed Alta Fay.

Before the doctor was ever able to speak, the air erupted. Mamma's pent up worry gave way to an explosion of wails of grief and acknowledgement. The sound was one that Phyllis had never known before and doubted that she was likely to ever hear again. Through her tears she saw Mamma kneeling beside her little sister's body. Mamma's head lay next to Alta's, and her hand softly, meticulously petted her forehead and arranged her fine, blond bangs. She talked sweetly and soothingly, as if Alta Fay could hear her every word.

"Oh, my good girl, my dear sweet baby," murmured Mamma. Bursts of grief surged periodically, and Phyllis had to hold her breath out of sheer fright. She never knew when the next outburst would come, but she knew it was inevitable. It set her teeth on edge and made her body so tense that she would later feel the strain in her muscles. The stunned and confused family watched the disturbing scene as if it were all a bad dream.

Hot tears streamed down Phyllis's cheeks in warm trails before they fell to the floor. Through this blur she watched as Daddy quietly approached his grieving wife. He hovered over her and enveloped her shaking body, as if he alone could suppress the intensity of her emotions. He pressed his cheek against the top of her head as he gazed longingly and lovingly upon his child. His strong, callused hand reached down and gently lifted Alta Fay's.

Tears were coming. He could feel that familiar pressure behind his eyes that he had known only in childhood, when he was still weak. He had an almost unbearable tightness in his throat. It was painfully constricting. He was the man, though, and men were not supposed to show their emotions. The man was to be a strong, capable provider for his family, so how could he now let them witness him break down? He did not feel that he had been providing well or that he could remain strong, especially now. His heart ached. Fathers are not supposed to let bad things happen to their children. A battlefield raged in his mind. Had he run faster…had he gone for the doctor sooner… All he could feel were the torturous attacks of guilt for not having been able to do something more.

Mary stirred slightly, and that shook George from his despairing thoughts. He lifted his cheek from her head, but never let Alta Fay's tiny hand drop from his gentle grasp. As Mamma stood up Daddy took her place beside their daughter's bed. He knelt onto the cold, hardwood floor, clasped his free hand into his other, leaving Alta Fay's safely and snuggly in-between. Such silence was never heard before this day in the Clayton home.

Daddy bowed his head as in prayer. Phyllis could see his body shaking with sobs. She felt pity for him. His tears made her uncomfortable because she had never seen a grown man cry. Phyllis did not want him to feel ashamed that she had witnessed him weep. Observing her father in this state brought tears to her eyes, and she began to cry. It seemed her weeping would never cease. Truth be known, she wanted to cry forever. Forever seemed to be the length of time it would take to shed every tear she had for her sister. Tears would not wash away the pain, but it was a soothing way to cleanse one's heart and provide the rest of the body with the strength to face another day.

Mamma called the children to her and hugged them close.

"I love you all so much," sobbed Mamma. They were so small and required a great deal of care. Their young minds could not comprehend what had happened. Phyllis joined the children but kept her eyes fixed on the scene that was taking place behind her Mamma.

Daddy's head was still bowed, and through the sniffling and murmurings of her siblings, Phyllis could hear him speaking.

She was surprised by what she heard because her father was not overtly religious. They neither prayed before meals nor spoke of faith as a family. Phyllis remembered her Daddy in a know-all manner saying, "I figure that if you believe in God and there isn't one you haven't lost a thing. But, if you don't believe in God and there is one, then you have a problem."

Phyllis knew from what her Mamma had taught her from the Bible that Daddy was wrong. He was blind toward the Truth. She loved her Daddy and prayed, "God, please draw him near to you. He doesn't know the Truth."

For George, it was not a matter of outright denial, but a matter of indifference. By default, Mamma had become the spiritual leader of the family. She brought her children to church every Sunday and tried her best to lead them down the narrow path of salvation. She saved and sent boxes of second-hand clothes to missions every year. Daddy never went to church. There was always something else that needed tending to.

"I'd be wastin' half a day of work if I went to church and you know we need the money," Daddy claimed.

He never criticized his family for attending church, and they, in turn, did not badger him concerning his nonattendance. Sometimes, late at night, Phyllis could hear Mamma discussing Heaven and Hell, Jesus and Satan, and the promise of the cross to Daddy. Phyllis did not know if he listened because she never heard him respond.

I can see the Truth so plainly. Why can't a smart man like Daddy see it? Phyllis wondered to herself. She meant to discuss the matter with Mamma one day.

Oh Lord, what have I done to deserve such grief? Daddy silently asked God. *How do I explain this to my children? Will my Mary be able to cope with this loss? We have both lost a huge part of our heart!*

Hear me, Dear Jesus! Hear my cry! I am weary with grief and yet I'm expected to be strong for the rest of my family. Daddy's desperate wails of despair mingled with thought quieted into a soft sob once again, and he laid his head on Alta Fay's quilt to hide his shame.

Mamma must have heard some of Daddy's conversation because she let go of the children and slowly turned around in confusion. Her demeanor gradually transformed itself as she gazed at the man she had held, not in richer, but always in poorer, in sickness, and now in the death of their sweet baby. Was this the same man she had married? Under the overwhelming weight of her commitment, she snapped.

How many times did I witness to him and he never so much as flinched, wondered Mamma in disgust. *Why did it have to take our daughter's death to make him wake up? I suppose now he'll start performing his God-ordained duty as the spiritual leader of our family. He left the burden of the spiritual rearing of our children to me for all these years. How dare he try and step in now and act as if he were some sort of Saint!* Mamma's anger was brewing like strong coffee on a roaring cook stove. Her pride was mixed with anger and hurt, clouding her better judgment. She was acting in competition with her husband rather than working together as a couple should.

For a moment she became herself again, and her tears began flowing. Mary walked directly to Alta's bedside and brushed the back of her worn hand across each of Alta's cheeks. She kissed her tenderly on the forehead for a long time. Finally, Mamma arranged the quilt around her beautiful child so that it was neat and warm on her cool body.

Once Alta Fay was tended to, Mary's emotional rollercoaster began to spiral downhill. Overwhelmed and confused, her mood, suddenly and drastically changed. She turned toward her husband with brow furrowed. Tears of anger swelled in her dark eyes. Before she could contain her utterances she blurted, "I told you it wasn't the flu!"

That first accusation opened a floodgate of pent up emotion, mainly anger.

Fists clenched and jaw set, Mamma continued, "I told you that we should get a phone put in! Everyone but us has one! You never listen to me. I know my children and I knew Alta was very sick. She'd be alive if it weren't for you!" It spewed out in one long, violent, drawn out utterance. Mamma's anger spent, she began to moan and sob again.

Daddy, head still down, took the unwarranted, untrue verbal lashing with great calm. He did not flinch, nor did he deny all of what Mary said; indeed, he was beating himself up as well. However, George did not agree with all of his wife's angry accusations. He knew Mary well and loved her. She was in pain, and it was his responsibility to remain strong for her throughout this great trial. Lord knows, these past few years he had not been as strong as he could have been. He wanted to try harder for his family and himself. He needed to listen better and maybe even try to get to church on Sunday.

After all, if what his dear wife had discussed with him were true, he realized that nothing could have saved Alta Fay if it was the Lord's will to take her. Still, it was difficult to shake the guilty feelings of, *What if…?*

For Daddy, every event of that fateful day played many times over in his mind. He would be haunted until his death over the loss of his beautiful child.

Phyllis stood at the foot of her sister's bed, absorbing the words Mamma had yelled at Daddy. She could not help but feel that her daddy did not deserve Mamma's verbal lashing. Unfortunately, Mamma's words had voiced some of Phyllis's own feelings. She knew that she too had judged her father unfairly and out of anger. Phyllis felt guilty of disrespect. Her father deserved better than that, and she was embarrassed by her thoughts. One day she would talk to him about this.

Moving closer to the head of the bed, Phyllis searched Alta's sleeping eyes, thinking, hoping that they would open, but knowing all the time that they would not.

Phyllis silently asked God why He had taken her so soon. She found herself quietly recalling her Daddy's conversation with God. *Is he beginning to understand?* wondered Phyllis. She dearly hoped it was so.

As Phyllis was leaving the room to check on her younger siblings, who had gone out to get ready for bed, she overheard Mamma finally whisper, "I'm sorry, George."

When she turned around she saw her mamma hug her daddy. Without a moment's hesitation he took her in his arms and silently held her. This was the only thing he could do for his grief-stricken wife. He was not a man of many words during good times, and he was even less so in times like these. For hours they stayed together next to Alta Fay's body. Their silence engulfed the house. Any conversation that took place was done in whispers. It was only right.

Later, Phyllis tiptoed quietly in to bid her own farewell. Her heart was about to break in two. She sat in silence for hours, rocking to and fro in her mother's rocking chair, recalling days gone by. Phyllis's mind was rich with memories, and she slowly became a part of them. She closed her eyes and leaned her head back because the movement was soothing. After checking on the other children, Mamma returned briefly and draped a quilt over Phyllis. The winter night had become chilly in the little house. Phyllis was unable to feel this chill because she had wrapped herself in a warm blanket of memories.

Chapter 18

Memories of Days Gone By

THE FAMILY HAD VERY LITTLE money, and every now and again Daddy would shoot a whitetail deer out of season for food. Mamma would cut it up and fill every empty jar she could find. Phyllis remembered Mamma canning venison in a big tin tub over a fire pit in the front yard. She used a large wooden lid that Daddy had made for her to cover the jars as they cooked. Mamma used this huge tub when canning because she could cook several jars at once.

At the same time, Daddy was busy in the backyard burning several stumps that he was unable to extract from the ground. It was the only way to get rid of them so that the dark, loamy land could be cleared and planted.

Nearby the children were playing in the grass when into the driveway drove an officer from the Michigan Department of Conservation. Alta Fay's quick, spindly legs sprang into action and she ran out back. "Daddy, an officer is here, hurry!" As soon as he heard Alta Fay he fairly ran out front, knowing that he'd been caught poaching. Instead, the conservation officer politely said, "Good afternoon, Ma'am," as he tipped his hat respectfully to Mamma, walked directly past her and the cooking pot and right out to where the stumps were burning. He casually stated to Daddy, "Our officers saw smoke from the fire tower and wondered what was going on. I just came out to check. Did you know that there is a burning ban in effect due to the dry weather?"

Daddy apologetically replied, "No sir, I wasn't aware of that. I was just tryin' to get those darn rascals out of the ground so as I could work it up for plantin'. I got a big family to feed, you know."

"I understand. Got five of my own. But we can't be startin' a forest fire in these here parts," said the officer.

"You're right about that, sir. I'm sorry about inconveniencin' ya. Havin' to chase down the smoke and all," apologized Daddy once more as he shifted nervously from one foot to the other.

"That's my job," said the officer as he and Daddy put out the fires. Daddy was more than glad to extinguish the smoldering stumps and walk the officer to his vehicle. He breathed a huge sigh of relief as he watched and waved to the conservation officer backing out of the driveway. By the grace of God, he had not looked into the tub. When Phyllis looked back, years later, she believed that the conservation officer knew that Mamma was canning an illegally killed deer, but he understood the tough times and knew the family needed the meat. He made a decision to look the other way. Right or not, she was thankful for those types of men because some families, such as hers, may not have survived the rough times.

Continuing to reminisce about lean times, Phyllis recalled the minnow incident. Daddy was out of work and the family was all real hungry, so he walked down to a nearby creek and caught a whole mess of minnows for dinner. He brought them to Mamma, and she cleaned and cooked them for the family. They all ate heartily, but for some mysterious reason every one of them became extremely ill. It was a terrible incident. Thankfully, everyone survived.

Phyllis remembered that Alta Fay, although very sick herself, helped out with the babies. They enjoyed her silliness between their bouts of stomach cramps. Alta Fay was a strong child. It is ironic that she would be the one to succumb to an illness. It didn't seem right.

A sudden chill brought Phyllis back to her senses, and once again she was back in the cold, dark room sitting next to the body of her little sister. The quilt Mamma placed on Phyllis while she slept had slid down to the floor and lay in a heap around her feet. She picked it up and set it on the chair, looked at Alta Fay, and then left for a few minutes in order to stoke the fire and add some more wood to it. When she reentered the room, she saw that Mamma and Daddy was back, along with Barbara.

For the next short while the three talked about Alta Fay's brief life. Phyllis only participated by listening. Gradually, the trio began to feel sleepy and the room quieted. Once more Phyllis drifted into her own thoughts of her dear sister. She remembered that there were ladies around the area who saved their flour sacks and gave them to Mamma. "You girls get in here and let me measure you for your dress," called Mamma. She fashioned these into garments as best as she could, because store-bought dresses were not affordable. Phyllis dreaded wearing this type of dress, although she kept her complaints to herself. Everyone knew who the poor kids were and they were often teased. These flour sacks had large stripes or a floral pattern printed on them because the companies who shipped the flour were sensitive to the fact that times were hard and families could use this material to make clothing.

Alta Fay never minded them. She wore hers as proud as if she had on a full-length ballroom gown. Phyllis pitied the person who attempted to jeer at Alta's attire! Alta Fay was quick-witted and would come back with a smart remark to put the person in his place. If that tactic didn't work, she would have been on the perpetrator like a cat on a mouse. Phyllis smiled as she thought that Alta Fay wouldn't mind being dressed in a flour sack for her burial. But the ladies from the church will find a beautiful, second-hand dress that Mamma will use. They had done that for the poor Hansen girl who had died from pneumonia last winter. Either way, Phyllis was confident that Alta Fay would have been content. That was just her way.

Again Phyllis smiled, only this time, even in the dimly lit room, Mamma noticed. "What are you thinking about, Phyllis?" she asked.

Phyllis repeated her thoughts but made sure not to hurt Mamma's feelings or cause her more grief and guilt. That was not her intention. Fortunately, Mamma understood. "Mammas know more of what their children are feeling than they let on," said Mamma.

"How do they do that?" Phyllis asked seriously. In jest, Mamma replied, "Mammas are magical. They have eyes in the back of their heads. Didn't you ever know that, Phil?" Mamma smiled. Phyllis stared in awe at her mother and was not about to dispute her claims. It was true that Mamma was wise to all her children did, and to most of what they were thinking. All this time Phyllis thought they had been clever, when they were all being read like a book. Phyllis was not offended that Mamma knew her so well. In fact, Phyllis's respect for her Mamma seemed to grow even more after this conversation. This is probably why Phyllis felt comfortable continuing with more of her thoughts; only she was now able to share them freely with her Mamma.

"Mamma, do you know how much Alta Fay and the rest of us hate to be treated for lice?" asked Phyllis.

Mamma smirked. "Do you think I enjoy that terrible job? No, thank you!"

Mamma would have to pour some kerosene or sulfur and lard mix onto a rag and repeatedly rub it into her children's scalps. Mamma continued, "It sure is a time consumin', smelly job!"

"I don't like havin' that stinky ole' kerosene soaking into you kids' scalps, but that is where those critters are most active and they have to be destroyed. No getting 'round that!" Mamma explained in more detail.

Mamma found that it worked best if she wetted their hair then combed out all of the "rats' nests" before she started with the kerosene. She learned this after the first few bouts with the pesky creatures.

Mamma gazed into the darkness as she continued, "Alta Fay was famous for having snarls because her hair was so very fine. She'd shriek out like a wild cat as I tried to get that darn comb through her tangled hair. It had to be done, though."

The conversation stopped abruptly for a few seconds. All that could be heard was the rocking of Mamma's chair. She seemed to become angry with herself for thinking about lice and other distracting memories, as her daughter lay lifeless in front of her. Again, Mary's mind became a raging, rambling battlefield, and she angrily began speaking aloud. "Darn you, Alta. I would be more careful to not hurt your tender scalp if you were here. Why'd this happen, God? I didn't get to be with her when she died. With your help, I brought her into this world, and you didn't let me be with her when she went out!"

Coming back to her senses, Mamma began to sob. Though she had already forgotten her outburst, grief and regret continued to exhaust her body and soul.

Phyllis brought her Mamma back by reclaiming her attention with a warm hug and a kiss on her weathered cheek. Then Phyllis continued, "Those lice are sure hard rascals to get rid of. It takes us forever to get them out of the bed sheets, pillows and anywhere we lay our heads down."

"Those nasty bugs cause me more work than I can handle with all you kids. It's just one extra thing needing tending to," Mamma softly replied as she wiped the tears off her cheeks.

Phyllis, having regained Mamma's participation in the present conversation, went on. "The worst part is the terrible smell of kerosene. It seems to take weeks before the smell goes away. Meanwhile, all of the kids in school are laughing at us and sayin' we're dirty."

"Well, they don't know a thing and don't let them be botherin' you no more. Anyone, rich or poor, can get those miserable bugs. You just wait, one of these days one of those who laughed at you will be getting their head soaked with kerosene," said Mamma, shaking her finger as if she were scolding someone. She knew how mean children could be. She maintained confidently, "What goes around comes around."

Mamma patted Phyllis on the forearm and rose once more and left the room to check on the other children and go to the toilet. Her slippered feet scuffed along the hardwood floor. The sound was so familiar it would become engrained in Phyllis's mind for the rest of her life. She closed her eyes, leaned her head back, and listened and thought.

One of the last memories that Phyllis had before her body was spent was that of two separate outhouse incidences. Daddy and some friends dug a new hole directly in front of the outhouse because the other had become full. Their mission was to push the outhouse forward so that it came to rest over the new hole and then they would bury the old, full one. However, it had gotten dark before they could finish the job. Unbeknownst to Phyllis, her father's plan was to begin the chore again early the next morning. As nature would have it, during the night Phyllis had to use the outhouse. It was a nice night and Phyllis thought, *Instead of using the pot and having to empty it tomorrow morning I'll just run out to the outhouse.* It was very dark, but Phyllis knew the way perfectly. However, like most children, she was afraid of the dark and thought, *I'll do my business and return to the house as fast as I possibly can.* From the back porch, Phyllis took off in a beeline sprint, but just before reaching the outhouse door she tumbled, head long, into the deep, dark hole. She could smell the freshly dug dirt. It felt damp and cool. Her left ear was filled with dirt and she had scraped the side of her face. At first she was in shock and then she remembered what had been done earlier in the day. Phyllis wasn't hurt, but she was scared. As she fell she must have screamed out because, in a matter of minutes, most of her family stood at the edge of the hole, gaping down at her.

"Are you all right, Phil?" Mamma inquired. Once the family was assured, they began to chuckle. Alta Fay had giggled a bit, but she knew that Phyllis's pride had been hurt. Daddy lay on the ground next to the hole. Reaching his hand in, he ordered, "Grab hold, Phyllis."

With one pull of his strong arm, Daddy had his daughter safely out. Alta Fay gingerly brushed the dirt off of Phyllis. She squeezed her sister's hand and pulled her to her feet. Alta Fay hugged Phyllis all the way back to the house. In the morning, Phyllis emptied the full pot.

However embarrassing this was to Phyllis, it was nothing when compared to the humiliation she experienced earlier that same summer.

There was an old barn behind the Clayton home. In this barn there was an old, basement-type manger, and in one corner, their father had placed a pole. This springy pole stretched from one corner to the other, hovering about three feet above the floor. George would use this as a makeshift outhouse because he could not stand the regular, smelly one that everyone else used.

One day, Phyllis, Alta Fay, Barbara, and Clare were playing in this old barn. Phyllis needed to use the toilet and decided to try out her dad's personal commode.

While she was going to the bathroom, she continued talking with her sisters, who were wandering about the barn. Phyllis sat there for quite some time, and, with each passing minute, she became more confident in her ability to balance. Thus, she decided that bouncing a little bit might be fun. She began to giggle as she bounced, and her sisters rushed over to see what was so funny. Bounce, bounce, giggle, giggle, crack! Silence. The entire catastrophe seemed to happen in slow motion. Phyllis had bounced and the long, springy pole cracked. It broke in the middle, and Phyllis fell into the human feces that were piled up on the manger floor. She gagged, began crying, and quickly groped her way out of the manger. As soon as she was out of the barn, she ran down to the well as the older girls followed, laughing hysterically. It was Alta Fay who rushed into the house, grabbed a bar of soap that their mother had recently made, and brought it out to Phyllis. She helped her wash until every last glob of the gunk was off of her body. She even washed Phyllis's flour sack dress and let her wear her good Sunday one until Phyllis's was dry.

BACK IN THE chilly room it had become late. Phyllis's body was both physically and mentally exhausted, and she finally dropped off into a fitful sleep. In her dreams Alta Fay was very much alive. She laughed and played like she had always done. In her sleep, Phyllis smiled. She was happy once again.

Chapter 19

Grief

BEFORE THE DOCTOR HAD LEFT, he said to Phyllis and her family, "I'll let the neighbors know what has happened. The road commission said they'd plow up to your folks' house tonight and let them know." The doctor put on his warm clothing and held his woolen hat. Then, before he stepped out into the cold night, he turned and spoke. "I truly am sorry Mr. and Mrs. Clayton. There was nothing more that I could have done for Alta Fay. She's in the Lord's hands now."

Grief

He placed his hat onto his balding head and used the earflaps to secure it in place. With that, he was gone.

In such a small community, word of Alta Fay's death would travel like wildfire. This would mean several days of neighborly aid would come to this fragile family in the small, worn-out home down the cold, snowy lane.

At the present, however, the V-Plow that was burrowing its way to Grandma and Grandpa Blanchard's was top priority. *It is most critical that they know firsthand,* thought Phyllis. She couldn't bear the thought of its impact on Big Grandma and Grandpa. Phyllis would know soon enough how accurate her youthful intuitiveness was, for the Blanchards had truly been dealt the most devastating blow of their lives. The plow driver's news, delivered a few hours later, shattered the hearts of this elderly couple.

There were no bells jingling on the shire's harnesses tonight. Life, in an instant, had changed. Grandma's worst nightmares had come true, and she was in shock. Grandma and Grandpa Blanchard headed, at the quickest pace possible, down to see their lovely grandchild and their grieving daughter and her family. The news had so shocked the elderly grandparents that they were speechless throughout the entire trip. They kept their glazed eyes forward and withdrew into their own worlds. Wild gusts of wind and snow stung their faces until they were chapped and raw, yet neither felt it. Big Grandma had a stocking cap pulled down over her disheveled hair. She had not bothered to brush it out. She had come to the door in her robe and nightgown to receive the tragic news, so the clothes she put on were thrown together as if she were a bum from the street. She was in such a rush that everything was mismatched, right down to her socks. It made no difference at this moment. She had to get to her children. Mentally she was clawing the air, like a mother digging her way through rubble to get to a trapped child.

The shires were not trotting quickly enough to suit Big Grandma, and she broke the cold, still silence by yelling over the wind, "Inez, you get these horses movin' or I'll take the reins, dang ya!" He shook himself out of his stupor, taking no offense at her abruptness, and snapped the reins obediently. Not once did his numbed senses allow him to think about the dangerous consequences of having the shires slip and fall.

Upon nearing the Clayton's home, before Grandpa could stop the team, Big Grandma was climbing down off the wagon. The moon was clouded over, yet enough of its light shone to brighten the too-white snow.

"Be careful, Agnes," cautioned Grandpa. She waved her hand back in a you-no-never-mind way. Up to the house she waddled more briskly than she ever knew she could. Grandpa was concerned that she may be pushing herself beyond what her body could handle.

"Come in, Ma," Daddy solemnly said as he stood in the doorway of the shack. He whispered, "Mary and the kids are in with…" He could not say "the body," yet he could not say "Alta Fay." One sounded so unfeeling and final, but the other made it sound like the child was just ill and in bed. Big Grandma did not need an explanation, and she hugged her son-in-law tightly. Then, Grandma bustled in and Daddy hurried out to help Grandpa take care of the shires. The barn would, at least, protect them from the wind.

Grandma quickly but quietly entered Alta's room. When she stared at her lifeless granddaughter lying beneath the quilt, she wanted to rush to her side and wake her up. *She is only sleeping. She cannot be gone,* hoped Grandma.

"Oh, Dear Mary, baby, oh, the Lord giveth and the Lord hath taken away!" cried out Big Grandma as she embraced her daughter, and together they sank to the floor beside Alta's bed, still holding one another and sobbing uncontrollably.

Heartache such as this Grandma had never known. Her body felt twisted and wrung out like a wet dishcloth.

I cannot live through this pain, Grandma thought to herself. She would have traded places with Alta Fay in a second. *I don't understand, God. Help me to understand. Help us all to understand why terrible things happen to innocent children.* Why, oh Lord, why? Grandma's body heaved with sobs.

After regaining some composure, Grandma left the room. It was too much for her to stay the entire time with Alta Fay. The more she looked at her, the more frustrated she became. Grandma should be able to fix her, but she could not. She was utterly helpless and it gnawed and tugged inside her.

So for many hours Big Grandma looked in on Alta Fay, hugged Mary, comforted George and her husband, and cared for the other children. Her mechanism for coping was in maintaining an intense level of busyness. If she were to slow down, her mind would ponder the recent, dreadful event again and again. This type of coping takes a heavy toll on one's body.

Big Grandma and Grandpa spent the night with their grieving family. Arrangements needed to be made, and they were there to help out in any way possible.

By noon the following day, the community was aware of Alta Fay's passing. George's friends from work spent the better part of the morning constructing a simple coffin out of rough-hewn pine boards. They sanded and painted the outside an angelic white. Its beauty was in its simplicity. Mamma cried as she lined it with one of her best quilts. When they positioned Alta Fay into it, her fair-haired head rested on a beautiful lace pillow that the ladies from the church had fashioned with great care. Indeed, the second-hand dress the ladies had found for Alta Fay was beautiful. The poor family could not have asked for anything nicer under the circumstances.

As family, friends, and neighbors paraded through the Clayton home to pay their last respects, Phyllis stood guard next to Alta Fay. *I cannot stand people, most of whom I have never before seen, gawking at my little sister,* thought Phyllis defensively. In Alta's short life, Phyllis had acted as her protector, and she certainly would not shirk her duty now.

The hours droned on, filled with low, sad murmurs. Phyllis was exhausted from her soldierly duty and wished for the funeral procession to end. But the closing of the lid would signify the end of her best friend's earthly life. The finality this brought made her throat start to close, making it difficult to breathe. The book had ended, but not in its usual way. Books she had known usually ended in a resolution. Most of the time this resolution left all involved living happily ever after. Phyllis thought she had never read a book that ended in such sorrow as this one. It didn't seem right. Neither Phyllis nor anyone else could change the final chapter. The book was closed. *How strange,* contemplated Phyllis, *I always imagined that Alta Fay would grow up and become a famous storyteller and writer. Her stories would have never ended this way. I am certain of that.*

The folding chairs lined the living room and were filled. The preacher, firmly grasping a worn, black leather Bible in his right hand, reverently walked to his position in front of the mourners. The large Clayton family and the Blanchards had seats reserved in the front. It made Phyllis feel shy and embarrassed that people seemed to be making such a fuss over her family. They were neither well-to-do nor famous in any manner of the word, yet today they were in the spotlight. Phyllis was uncomfortable. Her entire body was in its own turmoil, and she began to squirm. Phyllis's heart was broken, her eyes burned with tears, her stomach was tied in knots, and she felt that all eyes behind her family were bearing down upon them. The weight of this feeling seemed to push Phyllis forward in her chair. Even the back of her head felt strange, as if people's eyes were like long, bony fingers touching her hair, which tingled with their stares.

Holding a closed fist to his mouth, the reverend discreetly cleared his throat and captured the crowd's attention. For about thirty seconds, he did not say a word, but deliberately and slowly, with his eyes, scanned over the gathering. All eyes were fixed on him and one could have heard a pin drop.

"We are gathered on this solemn occasion to pay our last respects to the dearly beloved child, Miss Alta Fay Clayton, the fourth daughter of George and Mary Clayton," began the Reverend. "Her tiny body lies here," he said, emphasizing this by sweeping his left arm toward the casket. "But her soul is with our great Lord in Heaven, and for that we can rejoice," he continued, gazing skyward, his right hand reaching upward, toward the ceiling.

What do you mean, rejoice, thought Phyllis angrily. *How am I to rejoice when I've lost my sister and friend? Rejoice…Phooey!* Phyllis's forehead creased and she pursed her lips. As the Reverend continued and she listened more closely, her tense body relaxed. She was content hearing the reverend tell stories about Alta Fay. The more he talked, the more confident Phyllis was that he truly thought the world of Alta Fay, and he was sorry about her death. He knew her well, and his strength of leadership was a great comfort to the family.

As Phyllis sat quietly and the memorial sermon droned on, she recalled attending a funeral once for a man whom the preacher did not know. It was awful. There were no stories about this man's life, and the preacher kept pronouncing his last name incorrectly. *How embarrassing for this family,* Phyllis thought. It was truly pitiful. The entire service, though short, was impersonal and without much hope. Phyllis was grateful to Big Grandma and Grandpa Blanchard and Mamma for having brought all the children to church. *Alta Fay would not leave this earth with no one knowing who she was and what she was like. Our Reverend made sure of that. He wouldn't pronounce her name wrong, either. He saw her most every Sunday,* Phyllis proudly thought. In a way, the church was like an extension of the Clayton home. It was comfortable, and there was a church family that was willing and able to help carry the family's burden during their time of need. Phyllis wished that every family had that comfort. She wondered if Daddy felt that comfort as well.

When the service ended, the mourners filed out in reverent silence. The Clayton and Blanchard family were the last to bid their farewells. Each, in turn, walked to the casket. Big Grandma kissed Alta Fay on the forehead as her large, soft hand tenderly rested on Alta's small, cold hand. Tears streamed down her cheeks in hot trails and into the coffin. She stared intently at Alta Fay's tiny body as if she wanted to engrain every single detail in her mind forever. Then silently she walked away. She kept within her own thoughts for a long time, acknowledging friends only when directly confronted.

Mamma was different. She kissed and held Alta Fay's cheek and hands; tears flowed in great torrents into the coffin. Daddy touched Alta's hand and then attempted to bring Mamma away from the coffin. Mamma shook free, yelling, "Let go of me!" As she picked Alta up and held her again, Daddy fought her desperate attempts to hold onto their little girl. "You've got to let go, Mary. She's gone. There's nothing we can do. Let her go." Daddy's voice became soft and sensitive. This had an effect on Mamma, and she carefully laid Alta back down, but continued to hold the side of the white pine box. Mamma began to sob hysterically, and Daddy held her as she lingered. Phyllis's teeth were set on edge once again. *Mamma, don't do this. It scares me when you act this way,* cried Phyllis to herself. It was not anger she felt toward her Mamma, but a deep compassion. She was helpless in trying to comfort her.

It took both Daddy and Grandpa Blanchard to drag Mamma away. She would not let go of the coffin's side, and it jarred and shook Alta's body. When Mamma realized the disturbance she was causing, she became horrified and embarrassed simultaneously. She hesitantly let go of the coffin's side, but her arms stretched, reaching out to Alta Fay. She continued her attempts to get back to her baby, though her strength was waning. *What a terrible sight,* Phyllis thought, *yet what love and pain.* A Mamma's babies are not supposed to die before the Mamma or the Grandma. Mamma should not be burying Alta Fay; Alta Fay should be burying Mamma. That is the way it is supposed to be. In Phyllis's young mind, she was trying to make sense of the situation, when suddenly she recalled a story she had been told. *When shepherds have a difficult time bringing their sheep up the mountainside so that they can graze in better pasture, the flock is hesitant. Most will not budge from where they stand. However, when the shepherd picks up a lamb and carries it up the mountainside, the rest of the flock will follow.* Phyllis wondered if Alta Fay was that little lamb in the Good Shepherd's arms. Daddy had already seemed to become more sensitive toward the family. His heart softened.

After the service, the crowd slowly filed out of the house behind the pall-bearers. It was a crisp, sunny winter's day. Watching each step, being careful not to slip and fall, the men worked their way to the Lister's wagon. With great care they placed Alta Fay's coffin in the back. The men jumped in, two on each side to keep it stable. Grandpa and Grandma Blanchard drove their shires the mile to the cemetery for the graveside service. The McGrath family offered their team and large sleigh to carry the entire Clayton family. Packed together in the back of the sleigh Phyllis and her siblings stayed warm. They had traveled to this cemetery before, but not in such luxury.

George and Mary did not shelter their children from death or the dying. January, two years prior, the oldest of the Clayton children, Barbara, vigilantly remained at Grandpa Kingsley's bedside as he weakened daily, eventually succumbing to lung cancer. Barbara had accompanied her father to the cemetery so that the Kingsley plot could be found under the deep blanket of snow. This was the first time that Phyllis became aware of the typical, winter burial procedure. She had watched as the men shoveled the snow from the plot until they reached the hardened earth. Some years, Daddy had told her, when the weather was mild and people had not trampled around on the grave plots, there would be very little or no frost in the ground, so the digging of a grave was relatively easy. Sometimes, though, the men would need to shovel the snow and then build a fire on top of the bare ground to warm it up. The heat would bring the frost out of the ground where they needed to dig. It was a time-consuming, tiresome task.

Alta Fay's death in that frozen month of February allotted them no ease of duty. The grave had been dug, and Alta Fay, resting peacefully in her angel-white coffin, was lowered gently to the bottom. The reverend opened his Bible and read Mark 10: 13-16 (NKJV). "Then they brought little children to Him, that He might touch them; but the disciples rebuked those who brought them. But when Jesus saw it, He was greatly displeased and said to them, 'Let the little children come to Me, and do not forbid them; for of such is the kingdom of God. Assuredly, I say to you, whoever does not receive the kingdom of God as a little child will by no means enter it.' And He took them up in His arms, laid His hands on them, and blessed them."

The church ladies began to sing "Amazing Grace" and the small group joined in. Once finished, the people were silent as they filed by the grave, each saying goodbye in his own way. Phyllis was the last to leave. She didn't care who heard her when she spoke into the open grave. "I love you Alta Fay, and I will miss you more than anything. Please remember me. I'll visit you as often as I can." Tears flowed warmly down her cheeks. Mamma waited for her part-way back to the sleigh. When Phyllis reached her, they hugged and walked arm in arm to the others. The pallbearers waited until the family was out of sight before they filled in Alta Fay's grave.

The sleigh ride back home seemed to take but a few minutes because Phyllis's mind was whirring. It seemed as though everything concerning Alta Fay and her death had been difficult. In Phyllis's opinion, her sister did not die quickly. She suffered excruciating pain until the bitter end. The doctor combated a terrible storm in order to rescue Alta Fay, only to be defeated halfway to the goal. Even the very act of burying her was a difficult task. Phyllis shared this difficult burden of Alta Fay's death as if it were her own. She pondered, *Why does it feel as though I am trying to run through a deep river? I stumble. I cry. I sink like an anchor to the muddy bottom. The strong current drags me downstream. Sometimes I am close to drowning and I don't really care. But in the end, just when all hope seems lost, something pulls me to the surface. I catch my breath and keep on struggling through life. I can barely think about living without Alta Fay. I feel so alone. Who's gonna be there when I do something silly, like falling in the toilet pit?* Phyllis's questions, on earth, would never be answered to her satisfaction, but, with faith and hope, she had a reason to go on living. Even at the tender age of eight, Phyllis had come to know this well. It is hope that sustains life.

Back at the Clayton's home, the ladies from church had busily prepared a fine dinner in the tiny kitchen, and wherever folks could find a place to sit and eat, they did. It was nice that the whole Clayton family was allowed to be first in line to eat. Again, Phyllis felt important, at least for a few hours. After the meal, the crowd slowly dwindled. The last condolences had been repeated, and now the ladies were beginning to clean the kitchen. While the rest of the family gathered together in the living room, Big Grandma, Mamma, Barbara, and Phyllis insisted on aiding in the clean up. The ladies in the kitchen politely refused, saying, "Just sit at the table and chat. You've been through so much these past few days." Neither the Clayton women nor Big Grandma could argue with that observation.

None of the family in the living room spoke much. Two of the younger siblings squabbled a bit, but all else was silent. Daddy sat stone faced in his worn, leather chair. Phyllis was sure that he was asking himself again, *What more could I have done?* Knowing that an answer would not suddenly appear, he continued to stare, indifferently, as his young children played around his feet.

Back in the kitchen, Mamma was quiet. In her mind she questioned her motherly attentiveness. *Why hadn't I realized earlier how sick Alta was?*

Is my baby cold and alone? Oh, Lord, don't let her feel cold. Please hold her for me. I'm sure that she is with you, God, but I am her mother. I need my baby, Mamma silently acknowledged.

Other than the clanking kitchen sounds and low murmurings of idle chatter between the women, all was silent. One of the younger ladies, apparently bothered by this, sat her dish-drying towel and plate on the table and eased herself into a chair next to Mamma. Gently she covered Mamma's hand with hers. It was warm from holding the dishes that were taken from the scalding water. It felt good. This lady was uncomfortable with the silence and thought that words needed to fill the emptiness. She said in a soft manner, "I'm sorry about Alta Fay, but you have six other children. You can always have more."

Before Mamma absorbed this, an elderly lady chimed in, "Old Ellie Miller never could have children. You should feel glad that you have had so many. Oh, there is so much to be grateful for." Big Grandma wanted to ring this old lady's bell for being such a monkey-baboon, but she kept the peace for Mamma's sake.

The ladies' voices droned on and Mamma sat politely quiet. She had taken in some of what had been said, but she tuned the rest out and withdrew into her own thoughts.

She knew these ladies meant well, but what they said was not right. They knew nothing, really. They had never experienced what she was going through, and were just talking to fill the noiseless room, nothing more. In a way, it made her angry.

Mamma was eternally grateful for every one of her dear children. She would give her life for any of them. Like a waterwheel, Mamma's mind whirled: *Was this old lady telling me that I wasn't grateful for the others?* That thought, Mamma knew, was ludicrous at best. Surely she didn't mean it the way it had sounded.

The young lady sitting with Mamma at the table must have been an apprentice to the old lady who spoke so absent-mindedly. Mamma thought, *This lady assures me that I can always have more children. Well, Hallelujah! There's a revelation! (Mamma's natural humor resurfaced for a moment.) So, if one in the pack dies it can be replaced, like a dead battery?* Mamma's thoughts were sarcastic but seemed to serve a medicinal purpose. *If I have another child, does it take Alta Fay's place? That is like stealing to me. That was Alta's place and no one could take it from her. I don't want that – not ever. Can't you see, you ignorant girl, that it is my Alta Fay that I want? A thousand dearly loved children could not, and should not, replace my little girl.* Deep within her heart, Mamma knew these ladies were not trying to cause her more pain, and she was thankful that they could not hear her bitter and defensive thoughts.

Indeed, Phyllis was grateful that they could not hear her thoughts! During the few days of comings and goings, she heard so many times from dear friends and relatives, "I'm sorry about your sister" or "Let me know if there is something I can do." These kinds of comments were repeated until they were worn out. In her exhaustion, Phyllis became irritable. The words became meaningless babble to her, and she began to resent each time she heard them.

These well-meaning people would have been more than happy to help the family out if they called. But, Clayton pride might not ever allow that to happen. Phyllis believed that most grieving families would respond that way. Those who are grieving feel that people have already made so many accommodations and sacrifices in their time of need; to ask for anything more would show signs of dependence, weakness, or just plain laziness on the griever's part.

Phyllis promised herself that, if it was needed, she would urge Mamma and Daddy to call those who offered help. She also vowed that when she was able to comfort a grieving family she would call on them occasionally to see if they needed anything. That way they wouldn't feel like they were begging or weak. Phyllis wanted to make a difference.

It was late enough by the time the last neighbors and friends had gone that Mamma did not make dinner. There would be enough leftovers for a few days. This was a great relief to Mamma.

Chapter 20

Afterwards

DADDY STOKED THE FIRE AND Mamma tucked the children all into bed. Daddy also came in, kissed each of the children and whispered, "I love you" in each of their ears for the first time. Those three simple words meant the world to them. Daddy had changed. He had grown and was slowly becoming his children's hero.

It was difficult for Phyllis to lie next to where Alta Fay had so recently been. Already she missed Alta's giggles and nighttime stories. Many nights Daddy would yell for the girls to keep the noise down so the little ones could sleep. They would pull the covers over their heads to muffle the sound before they continued their silliness.

On the nightstand next to Phyllis's big, lonely bed was the old wooden music box that Grandma Blanchard had given them. She carefully wound it up and listened to the familiar tune in the blackness. "Softly and tenderly Jesus is calling, calling for you and for me..." All the while Phyllis remembered Alta Fay, and she began to speak to God. *Lord, I just wish I knew if Alta Fay was all right.* Phyllis wondered, *Is she happy where she is?* Before she could finish her thoughts and prayers, she noticed that the music box was gradually slowing down. Then it stopped altogether. Silence again. The room was like a void in space and time. The air refused to move. Phyllis stared into the empty darkness, scarcely breathing. It was a stuffy, suffocating kind of nothingness. Without warning, panic struck her like a tidal wave. He heart raced and her hands and lips were shaking. Her skin was clammy to the touch. Phyllis just knew that she was going to die right then and there, and that Mamma would call to her in the morning. When there was no answer, Mamma would come into the bedroom and find her third oldest daughter dead, just like Alta Fay. Phyllis fought to survive, but death is uncontrollable and unpredictable. She bolted from the bed and opened the window. The cold air rushed in. She breathed in deeply, letting it fill her lungs to their full capacity. Phyllis slowly breathed out and slid to the floor, crouching and cowering against the wall. She wrapped her arms around her shins and rested her forehead on her kneecaps. Phyllis wanted to be alone, but she didn't want to die alone. She prayed that God would come to her rescue. After about twenty fearful minutes, her symptoms lessened until she felt tired and ready for bed.

It was best for Phyllis to lie on her stomach. It seemed to press in on her tumultuous insides. She rested with her chin on her pillow, and eventually her body and soul relaxed.

The only sound was coming from within her thoughts, and miraculously these thoughts slowly became soft and light and peaceful. Her memories were like butterflies dancing, fluttering, and alighting on brightly colored wildflowers in a grassy meadow. Phyllis began to feel comfortable. Her fears subsided and memories resurfaced.

She recalled the night of the Christmas party when Alta Fay said so sweetly; *"I'd buy you a pocketknife if I could, Phil."* Alta Fay's whispers continued to consume Phyllis's mind. *"Where do deer go when they die, Phil? Big deer die all of the time, but not little deer. Why is that? It doesn't seem right. That fawn didn't even have a chance to live its life, Phil,"* Alta's questioning voice softly and tenderly began to fade like a mist in the air. Hot tears streamed down Phyllis's cheeks and soaked into her pillow as she continued praying. Finally, she drifted off into an exhausted sleep. She hoped that Alta Fay found the answers to all her many questions.

Her sweet voice;
Afar it
lingers;
Nearby it
soothes;

Her precious memory
swirls about me
like wisps of incense;
Its light, playful scent etched
deep within my soul
will remind me of Alta Fay
'Til time shall be no more.

Epilogue

SPRING BURST FORTH WITH NEW life. The waking ground was scattered with mud puddles and young children who were eager to splash in them. Piles of dirty snow melted quietly in the sun. Tulip and daffodil sprouts burst through the soil in greater numbers each day. The scents of the air were clean and refreshing, and it made one want to take in several, deep, long breaths. Nature was in the process of renewal, and it could not stop and take notice of the loss of a dear sweet child. Time marched forth with a deliberate and carefree attitude. The seasons of life were continuing on, and the Clayton's must do the same.

There were many grievous months for the Clayton family. Everyone experienced periods of unrelenting sadness. Mamma's loss was the most visible. At times her grief would become so overwhelming for her that she would walk to the cemetery and lie down beside Alta Fay's grave for hours.

Daddy was quiet and expressed his feelings through his talent of working with concrete. Phyllis thought that there was nothing in this world more touching than watching her Daddy chip away on a rectangular block of concrete, using hammer and chisel, in order to fashion the nicest possible gravestone for Alta Fay. He set his mind to the task and did not let up until it was completed. He was a hard-working perfectionist. Each night, Mamma would bring him coffee, then sit inside the shed on a bale of not-so-new straw, admiring his handiwork. When completion day came, Daddy had to summon all of his strength to load the stone onto the back of Grandpa and Grandma Blanchard's wagon. They had driven the shires down early that warm and sunny morning for this special occasion. The entire Clayton family crowded into the wagon bed, being cautious around the beautiful stone, smiling as they jostled and bounced down the bumpy dirt road to the Sand Creek cemetery.

Alta Fay would have thought her stone was magnificent.

The minute the wagon slowed, the older children jumped out and ran instinctively to Alta Fay's grave. They had quickly memorized the route. It took Daddy a while longer, carrying the heavy stone. Mamma held back and walked along with her strong husband.

"You really did a good job on Alta Fay's stone. She'd be so proud of you," Mamma spoke softly. "I'm proud of you, too, George. I love you." She rubbed the palm of her hand back and forth across George's back. He stopped briefly and lowered the stone to the ground. He stood up and stretched in order to catch his breath. Mary leaned her head affectionately onto his shoulder for a moment, and she draped her arm around his waist. Finally, he stooped, picked up the stone again, and they continued walking.

He didn't say much, but it was evident how proud he was of his work. His wife and children acknowledged his accomplishment, and it made him feel whole again. His kids still loved him. They looked up to him as if he were now their full-fledged hero.

Standing beside the rectangular cemetery plot, the children formed an aisle-way and allowed their father to firmly place the stone at the head of Alta Fay's grave. He pressed down on it as he moved it back and forth, making it as level as possible. Daddy stood up, stepped back, tilted his head slightly to one side and smiled. Mary and the children gathered around him, and they hugged each other for several minutes.

Standing in the background, Grandpa and Grandma Blanchard gave their children and grandchildren some space. Now they felt it was appropriate to approach the Clayton family. Grandpa placed his hand firmly on George's left shoulder and patted it several times. Then, turning away, he groped in his pocket for a handkerchief to wipe his eyes. George turned to his mother-in-law, who gave him a Big Grandma hug. Tears erupted like a volcano onto Grandma's shoulder. She was weeping as well. George was not a perfect man nor would he ever be, but the Blanchard's thought he was a wonderful son-in-law and a good father.

After several minutes of wiping tears and blowing noses, they all regained their composure and pitched in to arrange dainty spring wildflowers around the stone and smooth out

Epilogue

the dirt. Already tender shoots of grass were growing in thin patches. It would not be long until it all filled in and a beautiful, lush green blanket would keep Alta Fay warm. Once the final touches were made, the family turned and wandered back to the wagon. They stopped occasionally to observe several of their other relatives' graves.

The trip back to the Clayton home was quiet and the conversation was light. Grandpa Blanchard turned to address Daddy who was, at the moment, trying to keep his youngsters seated in the back of the wagon, "I know where some lilacs bushes are at. First chance I get, maybe we could go dig 'em up and plant 'em around the grave."

"Lilacs were Alta Fay's favorite springtime flower. Thanks, Inez," Daddy replied, gazing off into the distance. He sat quietly and thought about how much he loved his family.

Through the years Phyllis would come to the realization that her father was a man who kept his feelings bottled up inside him. At times she wished, for his own benefit, that he would share more of his thoughts with his family. However, Phyllis was not sure if he knew how to do this.

But all could not be counted as loss. George had grown closer to his wife and children. He decided to attend church with the rest of the family, and they were more than happy to have him accompany them.

The moments of sorrow were few compared to the many times throughout the years that the family would reminisce about Alta Fay while sitting around the dinner table or visiting in their living room. The aroma of hot, black coffee and the sounds of laughter filled the Clayton home. In this way, Alta Fay's memory was kept alive. This family's precious memories combined with faith gave them hope that one day they would be reunited with their beautiful daughter and sister, Alta Fay.

Like the soft back of a child's fingertips being gently drawn across my cheek,
the quiet breeze brushes against me.
Refreshingly cool, your precious memory breathes on me in the summer,
delightfully warm.
It wraps me up like a grandmother's quilt in the winter.

Memories of you fill my heart and mind.
Sometimes they sweetly lull me to sleep,
At other times they grip me like a vise pressing heavily upon my heart.
I ache for you inside;
An emptiness remains that can only be filled by you.

Oh how I love you, little one.

For a fleeting moment I hear your small, sweet voice calling to me as it playfully dances on the breeze.
And once again, precious memories gently brush their delicately, caressing fingertips   across my cheek.

Dear Lord, let that breeze never end.

Pen and Ink Drawing by Amber Ellis

Author's Note

GEORGE (DADDY) AND MARY (MAMMA) Clayton eventually had twelve children. Mary died November 11, 1969, as a result of complications from a head injury sustained during an automobile accident the preceding July. George died of old age in 1995.

Phyllis eventually married and had five children, one of which died at the age of two months. While her children were young, she obtained her GED and attended Mott Community

College in Flint, MI, where she earned her degree as a Licensed Practical Nurse. She worked, mainly in pediatrics, from 1958 until her retirement in 1985, at St. Joseph's Hospital in Flint. She was nominated for Nurse of the Year for Oakland University, after her husband of 51 years submitted a tribute to Phyllis's nursing career. The University's Nursing Professor was so moved by this heartfelt tribute that she asked permission to print it, in its entirety, in the Oakland University Paper. She wanted all of the student nurses to read it.

Ironically, during one of Phyllis's night shifts in the Pediatric Unit at St. Joseph's Hospital, she became concerned with a young patient. She knew that something was not right with this child. The interns on duty did not see any problems, but the gnawing feeling Phyllis had would not go away. She called the regular physician at his home, and he, trusting Phyllis's instincts, immediately rushed to the hospital. The child needed emergency surgery for a ruptured appendix. The child was critical for quite some time, but he survived. Had Phyllis recognized some of Alta Fay's symptoms in this child? She had helped save a family from a grief that she had known many years earlier. Phyllis had an angelic aura about her that attracted children of all ages. Phyllis's nurturing began early with the care of her siblings. She had experienced grief at a tender young age and was able to, for several decades, demonstrate empathy toward many others in similar circumstances.